Customer-Centric Marketing

Customer-Centric Marketing

A Pragmatic Framework

R. Ravi and Baohong Sun

The MIT Press
Cambridge, Massachusetts
London, England

This book was set in Stone Sans and Stone Serif by Toppan Best-set Premedia Limited. Printed and bound in the United States of America.

Library of Congress Cataloging-in-Publication Data

Names: Ravi, R. (Ramamoorthi), 1969– author. | Sun, Baohong, author.
Title: Customer-centric marketing : a pragmatic framework / Ravi, R., and Baohong Sun.
Description: Cambridge, MA : The MIT Press, 2016. | Includes bibliographical references and index.
Identifiers: LCCN 2015038402 | ISBN 9780262529051 (pbk. : alk. paper)
Subjects: LCSH: Relationship marketing. | Customer relations. | Marketing—Management.
Classification: LCC HF5415.55 .R38 2016 | DDC 658.8/12—dc23 LC record available at http://lccn.loc.gov/2015038402

10 9 8 7 6 5 4 3 2 1

Contents

Preface   vii

1   An Introduction to Customer-Centric Marketing   1

2   Conceptual Framework for Customer-Centric Marketing   15

3   Modeling Consumer Choice   33

4   Segmenting Customers into Latent Classes Based on Sensitivity   51

5   Customer Lifetime Value   65

6   Marketing Optimization Problem   77

7   Continuous Learning and Adaptive Marketing Decisions   95

8   Implications and Enablers   109

Epilogue   115

Notes   117

References   121

Index   127

Preface

The traditional orientation of marketing efforts have always centered on the campaign: new or revised products or services are released with an accompanying marketing campaign to meet goals of purchase. The advent of data collection and analysis techniques have helped hone the design and response of these campaigns to the immediate sales goals.

The revolution of big data and long data (that is historically rich, also called panel data) holds an entirely different and game-changing promise for marketing that is only beginning to be realized. Data technologies have enabled the asynchronous and continuous collection of customer interactions with a firm that carry rich signals about consumer preferences, consumption patterns and their changes. Rather than use the most recent, frequent or monetarily lucrative transactions with customers to determine whether they will be good candidates for a current campaign, the new promise is to make the marketing and sales process adaptive, dynamic, and responsive to the changes in customer patterns. In other words, rather than using only a temporally myopic view of the customers from this rich data collection to design campaigns, we advocate a longer view over time of following a customer's interactions to design a customer-centric marketing (CCM) plan. This is a deeper and more effective use of the data revolution in marketing.

This book is meant for business marketing leaders strategizing profitable growth for their companies. Many of them have been focused so far, particularly during the recession years beginning in 2008, on securing cost efficiencies. The productivity gains they have achieved through initiatives like supply-chain management have reached the point of diminishing returns. It is mathematically impossible for an organization to sustain cost advantages if its competitors are also taking an identical route to reach an identical goal. Cost-based management can only take a company so far and no further. What can, however, take a company far is its ability to gain and sustain a long-term relationship with customers as individuals. From this perspective, customer-centric marketing is a competence that is not replicable and is competition-proof.

This book can be used as a textbook to meet an increasing demand for the application of quantitative and analytical skills to facilitate sophisticated marketing decision-making. The content of the book is based on cutting-edge research in optimization and interactive marketing. The goal is to apply optimization tools to derive analytical solutions leading to customized, dynamic and proactive real-time marketing decisions, such as relationship pricing, promotion management, cross-selling campaigns and service allocation. This book helps readers learn how to develop state-of-the-art marketing strategies by using relevant analytical techniques. An early version of this book was used as a text for MBA courses at Carnegie Mellon University and Indiana University.

For practical application, four mini case studies are designed to help readers apply the proposed framework of CCM to real-world marketing problems. These real-world case studies provide students with an opportunity to practice problem formulation, develop problem solving skills and master analytical marketing tools to derive day-to-day marketing decisions. The framework described in this book is related to terminology that has emerged recently among marketing practitioners, such as customer relationship management, big data marketing, predictive modeling, business analytics, proactive marketing and customer lifetime value analysis, and one-on-one, interactive, and dynamic marketing.

We have provided numerical examples with spreadsheets to illustrate basic optimization primitives used in marketing. They include regression analysis to predict consumption patterns; discrete choice models modeling the choices made by customers based on the logistic function and estimating its parameters using the maximum-likelihood method; employing a sophisticated latent class approach to segmentation from marketing; setting up customer lifetime value (CLV) and solving the basic marketing optimization decision problem for a firm; using dynamic programming on a time-discounted utility model reflecting customer lifetime values to solve the marketing optimization model for the firm; and incorporating adaptive learning of latent customer segment membership using a Bayesian update framework into the dynamic optimization framework using observed interaction parameters. If all of these sound too general and complicated, be assured that they will cease to be so by the end of this book and will turn into your own friendly, analytical tools to implement customer-centric marketing in your own context.

This book is based on joint research developed at Carnegie Mellon University when both authors were on the faculty at the Tepper School of Business. We acknowledge the inspiration and generous support from Carnegie Bosch Institute and iLab at Carnegie Mellon University, as well as Cheung Kong Graduate School of Business. We thank all the TAs and past students of the Tepper MBA elective Optimization for Interactive Marketing, on which this book is based, especially Viswanath Nagarajan, Liye Ma, and Ziya Hydari, who served as TAs and contributed to developing the exercises. We thank Chandrasekhar Ramasastry, who helped us develop the examples at the ends of the chapters. We are also grateful to Professor Shibo Li, who used a draft of this book to teach a similar course at Indiana University, for his comments and suggestions as well as his contributions to the Excel spreadsheets.

All the examples and exercise worksheets described in this book are available online at mitpress.mit.edu/books/customer-centric-marketing.

1 An Introduction to Customer-Centric Marketing

Key Ideas

- Customer-centric marketing is a strategy with which a firm offers the right marketing mix (product, place, price, and promotion) to the right customer at the right time through the right channel. Its objective is to maximize the customer lifetime value of each individual customer by satisfying changing demands.

- CCM has the potential to generate a favorable response from customers, given their preference for personalized promotions.

- CCM introduces a forward-looking component into ascertaining consumer lifetime value.

- CCM facilitates optimal trade-offs between short-term marketing costs and long-term profits.

- In this book, we advocate that firms should use information from ongoing interactions and continuously learn about the preference of each individual customer and act on those learnings to maximize CLV. Our framework combines both data analytics and the decision-making process of a firm. This results in a sequence of customized and dynamic marketing mix decisions that, in today's highly interactive marketing environment, can be automated.

- The resulting marketing decisions are customized, dynamic, proactive, and experimental.

- The move to CCM is driven by the proliferation of detailed customer information gathering, increasing computing power, and real-time delivery of personalized marketing messages.

- CCM reconciles the two activities of mining the collected data and making marketing decisions simultaneously and iteratively.

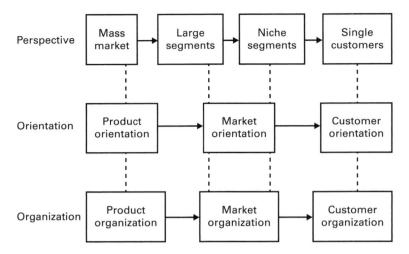

Figure 1.1
The growth of customer-centric marketing.
Source: Sheth, Sisodia, and Sharma 2000.

CCM: From Concept to Reality

Historically, marketing managers are used to holding "one-size-fits-all" mono-
logues with themselves. Of late, they are beginning to acknowledge the value of
holding "one-to-one" dialogues with each customer. The traditional archetype
of mass marketing, which viewed customers as a homogenous group with common needs, is being challenged by a new prototype of *interactive* marketing[1] that
views them as individuals with distinctive needs. Building relationships with
customers has become the new imperative.[2] Today, firms recognize that a closer
understanding of customer needs can be a source of competitive advantage. This
is a major shift in marketing paradigm.[3]

The shift is being triggered by the rapid expansion of the Internet and advance-
ments in digital technologies that are influencing marketing communications[4].
These advances transform data collection and storage technology into a system
that promotes service excellence and identifies revenue growth opportunities.[5]
The rapid decrease in the cost and effort of collecting and analyzing data enabled
by cloud computing and the ensuing accountability to make the data useful has
made this shift imperative.

The responses from marketers to the ongoing shift are varied. Some are
beginning to reconfigure their established practices. Some are beginning to

deliver fewer but more relevant messages to customers. But, many are finding it difficult to make the transition to CCM. This book is meant to help them find their way.

What Is Customer-Centric Marketing?

CCM means putting a customer at the center of a firm's marketing strategy. Marketers assess the needs of each customer individually. They ascertain when a customer needs what product, through which channel, and make a determination of how best they can meet those needs. They also take a call on related issues: (1) whether to serve that customer directly or via a third party; (2) whether to create an offering that customizes the product or standardizes it; and (3) whether to tailor other elements of the marketing mix.

Why Customer-Centric Marketing?

The answer to the question is an economic one: Because it will increase profits.

The move to CCM will happen for some of the following reasons.[6] First, customer resistance to intrusive marketing is increasing.

- 68 percent of customers agree there are too many advertisements today
- 66 percent of emails received are unsolicited

Second, customers are taking control from marketers.

- 75 percent of customers have signed up or intend to sign up for Do-Not-Call lists
- 74 percent have installed or intend to install pop-up and spam blockers

Third, marketing initiatives are becoming more effective.

- Customer-focused (as opposed to product-focused) communications will increase customer loyalty and, as a result, customers will buy more over a longer period of time

Fourth, marketing initiatives are becoming more efficient.

- Marketing investment will be better aligned with customer profit potential and fewer marketing dollars will be wasted on low-potential customers

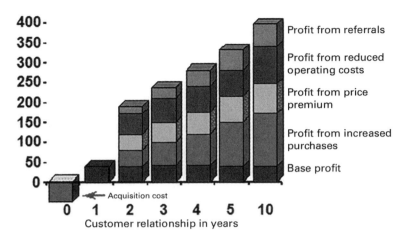

Figure 1.2
Company profit index.
Source: Cutler 2005.

How Are Customer-Centric Marketing Decisions Made Differently?

Most recent marketing practices are still campaign-centric. Their focus is on selecting the most profitable customers for a scheduled marketing intervention. CCM, on the other hand, recognizes customer heterogeneity, identifies the variables in relation to the cost of serving an individual customer and customizes the offering to suit the preferences of each customer. The goal is to acquire, nurture, and retain customers to maximize their lifetime value, while also controlling costs.

CCM thus requires management to incorporate three components into their decision-making process: (1) *learning* about customers, which identifies individual customers, follows their evolving demand and tracks changes in their preference;[7] (2) *forward-looking* orientation, which helps predict a customer's future reaction and profit implications of current marketing interventions;[8] and (3) *dynamic optimization*, which intertemporally trades off long-term revenue contributed by customers with short-term marketing costs, and results in customized, dynamic, and proactive marketing treatments.[9]

Customer knowledge involves tracking and predicting the needs of each customer at each stage of their evolution (*learning*).[10] Customer needs develop over time with changes in one's life-stages, accumulation of consumption experiences, available financial resources, and awareness of particular products. The firms would like to know an individual customer's readiness to consume a particular product—when a customer needs what product at what time and which is the best communication channel to deliver the message. In addition, the firm should know how the effectiveness of marketing mix decisions differs across different segments of customers and how the segment membership is characterized by customer demographics. In other words, learning involves developing insights on (at least) predicting customer choice, clustering customers based on their heterogeneous sensitivities to marketing mix, and profiling customer segments with identifiable signatures.

Foresight means identifying the future profit potential of each individual customer (*forward-looking* orientation). Marketing is an important part of long-term customer relationship management with the goal of maximizing total profit throughout the customer lifecycle.[11] This requires the firm to be able to follow the evolution of customers' needs, to predict their customers' future profit potential, and to be willing to forgo short-term profit in order to maximize long-term profit.

Dynamic optimization yields the optimal choice among strategic decisions around *who*, *when*, *what*, and *how*. First, the firm needs to integrate its knowledge of the evolution of demand maturity with customer heterogeneity. Then, it should predict the dynamic consequences of its marketing offers. Next, it should factor in the cost of customer acquisition and the contribution of a household to the firm's long-term profit, and last, it should make an optimal trade-off between short-term solicitation cost and long-term financial payoff.

Accordingly, a firm implementing CCM takes two iterative steps:

Step 1 *Learning about individual customers*: It continuously gathers new information about each individual customer and develops insights about the customer by analyzing results from the most recent interactions with the customer.

Step 2 *Acting upon customer information*: It acts on customer information by continuously updating its decisions in tune with the updated knowledge about each customer.

The first step involves learning. The second step involves taking action using a forward-looking dynamic optimization. Both are integrated and interdependent in our proposed framework.

The Four Salient Features of Customer-Centric Marketing Decisions

Our proposed framework results in CCM decisions that have four features.

First, the decision should be *customized*. This is because learning enables the firm to improve its knowledge about an individual customer and make marketing offers according to its best knowledge about that customer's preferences. While recognizing the evolving needs of each customer, our solution recommends the most appropriate marketing offers that best match individual customer preferences. For example, because we understand college students prefer email and social media as campaign channels, our solution helps adopt the most effective campaign vehicle, tailored to the preference of the young crowd.

Second, the marketing intervention is *dynamic* because it recognizes the evolution of individual customers and follows each stage of customer demand maturity and intervenes with the most appropriate marketing tool. Thus, two customers with the same demographic profile but different purchase history will receive different treatments.

Third, it should be *proactive*. This is because by following the development of each customer, and forecasting the effect of today's marketing intervention on future profitability, the firm can take preventive actions to avoid losing the customer. It implies that the firm can sacrifice short-term profits by offering customers their preferred choices to prevent defection and improve long-term profits. For example, offering the student customer a no-fee credit card account early in her career could potentially earn her loyalty over a long period. As another example, since we recognize the educational role of cross-selling campaigns by treating them as part of an integrated multistage process instead of as a promotion that triggers immediate purchase, our framework differentiates short-term, unprofitable customers from those who are profitable in the long term. Students are an example of a segment that may not be profitable today but have a long-term profit potential for a firm.

Fourth, our proposed allocation decisions are *experimental*. Testing whether a student customer is a sound candidate for an eventual home loan can be accomplished by offering her a small educational loan during her study tenure and monitoring her payment behavior.

What Fuels Customer-Centric Marketing? Information Drives Personalization

Firms have accumulated vast amount of data with transactional history in their IT systems. They have been able to infer customer choice behavior across service plans more carefully. There are several moot points, however. How can a firm use the data to more profitably price its service plans? The recent move toward big data and cloud computing, which make the collection, storage, and access of information regarding each interaction very easy, has fueled the trend toward customer-centricity. Given the central role of personalization in moving toward customer-centricity, firms from all types of industries, ranging from manufacturing to online retailing, are exploring innovative ways to accumulate and understand customer information.

Sophisticated data warehousing, data collection, and data mining tools offer promising means of gaining detailed knowledge about each customer. Big data marketing, data analytics, and data mining are drivers of new marketing initiatives that enable firms to retrieve the most recent customer information instantly and learn about the preferences of individual customers. More and more sophisticated statistical approaches are being developed to identify customer heterogeneity[12] without explicitly deriving firm decisions. Most of them provide a snap shot segmentation of customers, leading to methods that score or rank customers based on relevant variables. These segmentation methods are useful tools for *campaign-centric marketing*, which maximizes the return of investment of each campaign event by treating them independently over time.

However, data mining tools, no matter how sophisticated they are, only help firms understand the current snapshot of the customers and provide a foundation for making better immediate marketing decisions. In order to fully realize the value of detailed customer information collected over time and to profit from it, a firm needs to act upon the 360-degree knowledge of each individual customer derived from data mining tools and tailor its promotion, advertising, and product design to the most updated customer insights. In other words, acting over time on detailed customer insight represents the ultimate step toward CCM.

Today's technologies, such as mobile app capabilities, allow firms to deliver marketing decisions that are tailored to each individual customer in real-time. These technologies have created a demand for analytical marketing solutions that enable firms to act on customer insights learned from data mining and to generate marketing messages in response to individual customer actions.

Reconciling Data Analysis and Decision Support Systems: Our Key Idea on Customer-Centric Marketing

The approach we propose in this book explicitly treats firms as decision makers acting optimally on insights gleaned and updated from analyzing customer data continuously. It outlines a long-term model that tracks the firm's continuous interaction with the customers effectively and efficiently. More specifically, we formulate marketing interventions as solutions to a stochastic dynamic programming problem for the firm under demand uncertainty. We demonstrate the need for a firm to learn about the evolution of customer demand, the dynamic effect of its marketing interventions, the heterogeneity of customer preferences, the cost of interventions, and the long-term payoff, with the goal of maximizing the long-term profit of each customer. Our approach offers real-time solutions for integrating database querying and marketing decisions. It also provides a conceptual basis that marries the best of data mining with a real-time decision support system.

We discuss the two-step procedure ("learning" and "acting upon customer information") and the three components for CCM (learning, forward-looking, and optimizing) in more methodological detail. We use four cases to demonstrate the input, output, and benefit of our proposed framework. We also develop numerical exercises available in the online supplement to this book as Excel spreadsheets to illustrate the four ingredients of our framework (choice model, segmentation, customer lifetime value, and dynamic optimization).

Leveraging the Computing Advantage

Recent technological developments have opened opportunities to advance and automate customized and dynamic marketing decisions. Also, extraordinary increases in computational speed allow sellers to use more sophisticated tools to quickly analyze traditional databases and to continuously improve targeting strategies.[13] Thus, the fast paced development of online and direct marketing industries has created enormous opportunities for learning and real-time marketing decision making. However, there is substantial need for developing a real-time marketing decision support system that integrates the results of statistical algorithms for measuring customer insights.

In response to the growing demand for integrated data mining and analytical decision tools, some pioneering software applications have surfaced, that allow real-time marketing decision making based on customer information. Known as customer relationship management (CRM) or web analytics (WA), these applications allow firms to automate their data mining and decision-making processes. For instance, the On-Demand Customer Relationship Management by Salesforce. com claims that the software provides "point-and-click customization that fits the way you sell" and that "real-time analytics empower your business to make better decisions." The Microsoft Dynamics CRM 3.0 Professional Datasheet claims that it "is a complete customer relationship management solution that provides all of the tools and capabilities needed to create and easily maintain a clear picture of customers from first contact through purchase and post-sales."

The CCM decision-making paradigm calls for even more advanced software applications that integrate data mining and analytical decision tools more seamlessly. For firms experiencing difficulties in automating the implementation of customer-centric decisions, the statistical properties derived from our proposed framework provide guidance for managers to adjust their day-to-day marketing decisions.

Skills to Master

- *Define CCM and differentiate it from campaign-centric efforts.*
- *Describe its two steps (adaptive learning and proactive marketing decision making), three decision components (learning, forward-looking, and dynamic optimization) and four salient features of its results (customized, dynamic, proactive, and experimental).*
- *Identify examples of firms that have moved to CCM and their motivation and results from doing so.*

Examples

> At the end of each chapter, we list two examples to show how current company practices have incorporated some of the properties of our proposed solutions. The four mini cases, the chapter exercises, and the practice Excel sheet offer more complete demonstration on how our proposed framework can help unlock the potential of integrating detailed data analysis and decision support system.

Harrah's Entertainment Fine-Tunes Databases

The casino industry worldwide is competitive. Customers have many options in terms of how, where, and when they gamble. They also have entertainment alternatives outside the industry, like beaches, parks and resorts, contending for customer time. The single largest limitation for the management of a casino firm is that the customers are erratic in their loyalty. Locking in customers and maximizing their profit contribution over a lifetime is therefore acknowledged to be a key success factor in the casino business.[14]

Harrah's, a major US casino firm, had an ongoing customer retention program called Total Rewards, which it refined with technology inputs in a bid to address the critical issue of holding on to its customers. The approach was three pronged—tracking customer behavior, predicting customer behavior, and making targeted offers.[15]

It was classic CCM.

Historically, casino firms designed grand marketing schemes and tweaked their existing databases around them as an afterthought. And their reward schemes were based on the conventional retail wisdom: "Let's build it and they will come." Harrah's took a contrarian route with regard to both those trends. It mined its database first before designing promotional schemes. And its customer retention model was built on a belief that, "If we *know* our customers better and better, they will come more and more."

Harrah's had sixteen million members in the Total Rewards program that it had been running since the 1990s. On mining their transactional data, Harrah's realized four factors. First, it was deriving a major share of revenues, amounting to over 87 percent, from the casino rooms, rather than from the stores, restaurants, bars, or shows in its various properties. Its core customers were slot players, rather than entertainment seekers. They were responding better to an offer of $60 of casino chips than to a free room, two steak meals, and only $30 worth of chips because they enjoyed the anticipation and excitement of gambling. Second, its best customers were ordinary people with discretionary income rather than the gold-cuff-linked, limousine-riding high rollers on whom the casino industry, in general, had been fawning for years. Third, 26 percent of slot players who visited Harrah's generated 82 percent of its revenues. Clearly, they were its best customers and had to be pampered and cared for. Finally, its best customers were spending only 36 percent of their annual gaming budgets at Harrah's. It pointed to an opportunity for an upside in revenue.

Harrah's started refining its Total Rewards program by centralizing customer information, (such as name, age, social security number, and address) collected from various sources like websites, hotel front desks and call centers. The company learned that 75 percent of its transactions were being routed through the Total Rewards program, providing the core customer pool. Harrah's tracked the play history of each customer in terms of parameters like preferred locations, favorite games, playing time, size of bet, and number of bets. Based on the data it gathered, Harrah's sliced its customers into 80–100 segments for each property. It used segmentation as the basis to build a gambling profile of each customer. The profile enabled Harrah's employees, in turn, to offer a level of service that was not only unique to each customer, but, irrespective of the location of the property, uniform and consistent.

Central to Harrah's customer retention strategy was the database technology that enabled the company to estimate how much money it could theoretically earn from a customer over a projected period of time—CLV. Harrah's recognized that offering clear value propositions to core customers and cultivating lasting relationships with them would lead to greater and more sustainable growth not only in revenues but also in margins. Rather than track the amount that a customer would spend in a single transaction, Harrah's decided to predict their CLV and then appeal to their individuality in a bid to retain them. Its data analysts developed quantitative models that enabled them to forecast CLV for each customer with a degree of accuracy that was novel in the casino industry.

Harrah's then tapped into the basic human nature of aspiring to higher levels of achievement by categorizing its members into three tiers—Gold, Platinum, and Diamond—based on their ascending CLV. Gold customers stood in lines at the reception desk, or at the restaurant. Platinum customers would stand in shorter lines, and Diamond cardholders would rarely ever have to stand in line. The segmentation created a visible differentiation in customer service and mobilized an aspiration to move up the chain. Every experience in the casino was redesigned to drive customers to want to earn a higher-level card.

Harrah's also set up a series of automatic triggers in its database that would alert the system to provide appropriate responses that were consistent with the customer's stage in the value chain. For example, if a customer who was known to spend $1,000 per month with Harrah's hadn't visited it in three months, the system would generate a letter or telephone call to invite the customer back into the casino. If a customer had lost money during the last visit, it sent out a personal invitation for a special event. Harrah's telemarketers were also trained to listen for responses to specific offers and tailor the invitation accordingly.

To this day, Harrah's still fine-tunes its databases and marketing campaigns. They are considered works-in-progress. The company reviews the data on metrics, like offer acceptance rates, to assess the effectiveness of its marketing campaigns and provides feedback to individual properties to tweak the campaigns locally.

Loblaws Supermarkets Makes Digital Connections with Customers

A leading Canadian grocery retailer known for its President's Choice private labels, Loblaws Supermarkets had an ongoing customer retention program for several decades, around its plastic card known as PC Financial credit card. The program rewarded repeat customers with points that could be redeemed at the company's retail stores for a proportionate reduction in their grocery bill. An accumulated credit of one thousand points reduced the bill by one dollar at the checkout counter.

In mid-2012, the company realized, from mining historical data, that while its core customers, numbering six million, accounted for more than 60 percent of its revenue, it was capturing only 50 percent of their annual grocery spend. The data showed up an opportunity to increase the share of the wallet of its most loyal customers.

Therefore, in early 2013, Loblaws unveiled a new version of its customer retention program targeted at precisely that segment. Called PC Plus, it was a digital app[16]designed for smart phone users whose proportion of its loyal members was on the rise. The app was backed by algorithms that measured what an individual customer bought regularly, monitored the purchase record, and provided the most current profile of each customer. The algorithm was built to influence the shopping behavior in a bid to ultimately increase the value of its best customers. It used two metrics to track the shopping behavior: frequency of shopping trips and basket size of each trip.

PC Plus delivered coupons on smart phones, averaging a total of eight to ten products, every week. The coupons would not be for products that Loblaws wanted to unload but for products that the system had determined each customer wanted, based on purchase record. The coupons were aligned with the shopping patterns of an individual customer. No two customers got the same coupon, since no two customers had the same shopping behavior. This was the unique attribute of PC Plus.

Grocery retailers competing for a share of the customer's wallet with Loblaws had no clue about the promotional offers of Loblaws. They could not come up with matching offers since the offers were one on one. There were no flyers that could be seen by everyone, either online or offline. Personalization of coupons became a competitive advantage for Loblaws that competitors could not match.

PC Plus differed from its predecessor plastic card program in the way it incorporated the threshold value of purchase as eligibility for incentives. The threshold was personalized for each household; it was not uniform for all households.

It was well known, for example, that a single-person household would spend less on weekly or monthly groceries than a large family. The threshold was set for each household in a way that Loblaws secured just that spending stretch from customers at each shopping trip—without either making them spend beyond their means or incentivizing them for what they were already spending.

PC Plus deployed what was called "time to event modeling" wherein the system could automatically figure out when a particular customer might need to stock up on particular items. If someone bought, for example, Tide laundry detergent every twelve weeks, that person would be delivered an offer on Tide detergent shortly before he would normally purchase Tide. Conversely, if he bought, for example, Coca-Cola all the time, he would not be sent an offer on Pepsi.

But the system also had a provision for "stretch offers" that were promotions on products in which the customer would have indicated a passing interest at some time. Spot offers were also made with a view to step up the shopping frequency. A customer might be told that she would get additional reward points if she spent $20 in the meat department in a particular week. Or she could get extra points by shopping at her local Loblaws store five times within a particular month.

PC Plus brought several benefits to Loblaws. It enabled its store managers to target their promotion budget toward their best customers and their preferred categories rather than diffuse it across generic customers and generic categories. Each promotional coupon took into account variables like grocery spend and purchase pattern at the store that were updated with each transaction. PC Plus enabled store managers to drive incremental sales and comparable growth one customer at a time and one transaction at a time. It reduced the cost of not only promotion and advertising but also, significantly, market research.

PC Plus brought several benefits to consumers. It reminded them when the stocks of their favorite and regular purchases would start running low in the household. The coupon showed up on the smart phone on a prompt, preempting the need to carry the coupon to the store. The app helped them plan a visit to the store better by being served with a customized shopping list. It was significant in view of the finding by Loblaws that only 30 percent of all shoppers came to its stores armed with a shopping list. A ready shopping list served as an incentive to visit the grocery store. The shopping list was programmed in the order in which the customer would go through the store sections, starting with fresh produce first.

By end 2013, PC Plus had doubled the response rates to its coupons. It had also penetrated one third of Canadian households. Loblaws was working on bringing several improvements in its next generation customer retention program. The program would be redesigned to make the offers real time, rather than weekly. Customers would receive relevant coupons on their smart phones while cruising along the retail aisles of the company's stores with their shopping carts. The program would also involve vendors so that their supply chains would be integrated more closely into Loblaws demand forecasts.

Grocery retailing was a low-margin business worldwide. An ability to deliver consistency was a key success factor in the business. Consistency was being achieved through process standardization that also helped scale up efficiencies and improve margins through the cost reduction route. Loblaws was using the PC Plus as an additional route to improve its revenues and margins through a better understanding of customer behavior. PC Plus was also a route to influence customer behavior in its favor.

2 Conceptual Framework for Customer-Centric Marketing

Key Ideas

- Implementation of customer-centric marketing requires four ingredients tied together in an optimization framework: choice models, segmentation, CLV, and adaptive learning.
- Choice models and segmentation support learning about the customer while CLV and adaptive learning bolster the forward-looking component. Putting them all together in a dynamic optimization model completes the picture.
- Four case studies summarize real-life applications of the idea.

A Framework of Proactive Customer-Centric Marketing

CCM helps decide *when* to contact *which* customer with *what* product (or content) and *how* (in terms of the choice of communication channel).

In the following, we use the indices i for the customer, j for the product, k for the channel, and t for the time. The firm's marketing intervention decisions are solutions to a dynamic control problem under demand uncertainty with built-in customer reactions represented as maximizing the customer lifetime value:

$$CLV = \max_{A_{ijk\tau}} \sum_{i=1}^{I} \sum_{j=1}^{J} \sum_{\tau=1}^{T} \delta^{\tau-t} \, Prob\,(CHOICE_{ijk\tau} = 1)[REV_{ij\tau} - COST_{ij\tau} | INFO_{ijk\tau}, A_{ijk\tau}]$$

In the expression above, $Prob(CHOICE_{ij\tau} = 1)$ represents the probability that customer i purchases product j at time τ. We will model this using a predictive choice model based on the customer's utility. $REV_{ij\tau}$ and $COST_{ij\tau}$ are the revenue contributed and cost incurred for consumer i at time τ related to product j. The symbol *INFO* is a variable that keeps track of all past marketing actions as well as of the demographic information of the customer. $A_{ijk\tau}$ is the binary decision to be derived from the dynamic optimization problem on whether to offer customer i the marketing offer related to product j at time τ using communication channel k. In this book, we will consider continuing profits only from customers who are retained until period τ, so we will usually have $Prob(CHOICE_{ij\tau} = 1) = Prob(JRET_{ij\tau} = 1)$, where the *JRET* denotes the joint probability of having retained the customer all the way from the beginning period t until the current period τ. If we denote the probability of retention of product j from customer i at time period Θ alone by $Prob(RET_{ij\Theta} = 1)$, and assume that these individual period retentions are independent of each other, then $Prob(JRET_{ij\tau} = 1)$ will be product of $Prob(RET_{ij\Theta} = 1)$ for Θ ranging from t through τ. The objective function *CLV* represents the total customer lifetime value of the current customer base of I customers, across the range of J products, over a time horizon from the current time t until T, the end of the planning period. The optimization problem is computed in a forward-looking way for a time horizon of $T - t$ periods. The value $\delta < 1$ represents the usual one-period time-discounting factor in valuing future payoffs.

In the above equation, we set up the proactive CCM problem: At the beginning of the current time t, the company observes information set $INFO_{ijkt}$ consisting of past history and demographic variables that influence the choice utility and hence the choice probability of customer i for the product j in the current time t as well as the past interactions with the customer via channels k. Based on the accrued information, the company updates its belief on this customer's current utility according to a prespecified learning rule. Given this updated knowledge of a customer, the company calculates the total expected cost and revenue resulting from each possible CCM decision for all time periods from time t until the end of the planning horizon. With expected profit being defined by the above equation, the company chooses the best CCM decision that maximizes the expected long-term profit captured in the CLV expression.

From the figure, it is easy to see the learning, forward-looking, and dynamic optimization components of the process. The CLV objective allows the firm to implement the optimization problem over a long term rather than in a myopic, one-period fashion. The inclusion in the CLV of future revenues and costs that, in turn, incorporate future behavior of customers, imposes a forward-looking orientation to the optimization problem. Finally, having a component that uses information up to the current moment in changing the utility function of the customer along her lifetime enforces active learning in the process.

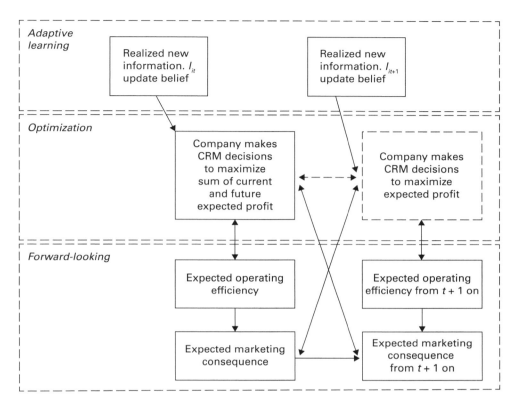

Figure 2.1
A temporal framework for proactive customer-centric marketing.

Four Modeling Ingredients

In this chapter, we explain the conceptual ingredients of the overall framework for interactive CCM. Recall that the three main decision components of the customer-centric approach are *learning* about customers, being *forward-looking* about their value, and using *dynamic optimization*. These three decision components can be implemented by using the following four modeling ingredients, which we will cover in one future chapter each.

1. Customer choice models

2. Segmentation based on customer sensitivity and adaptive learning

3. Customer lifetime value

4. Dynamic optimization

The first ingredient describes how customers make choices among brands, channels and products and how these choices are related to the firm's marketing mix decisions. Customer choice modeling is a widely studied area in marketing[1] that aims to develop statistically rigorous models of how customers make choices.

Segmentation helps identify and target appropriate customer segments for niche products. In our treatment, however, we will use segmentation in an expanded context. We segment customers based on their heterogeneous sensitivity to marketing mix variables such as price and quality. Furthermore, we profile customer segments based on their demographic characteristics. Later in the book, we will allow the learning aspect to incorporate the feedback of the change in customer behavior in response to the firm's most recent strategy: this is the key feature of adaptive learning that we advocate.

CLV is the time-discounted value of a customer to the firm calculated over the various revenues and costs associated with the purchases, servicing, promotions and other retention actions for this customer.[2] CLV serves as an effective optimization objective for the firm to use in making the company decisions, allowing the incorporation of customer choice models and segments, as well as learning effects.

Finally, solving the dynamic optimization problem so as to maximize the CLV of the current profile of customers (along with future attritions and additions) gives the optimal strategy for the firm to follow. This completes the picture of putting together all these ingredients that implement the three key decision components of CCM.

Applying the Customer-Centric Marketing Framework

By solving the CLV optimization problem, we can obtain a sequence of optimal CCM intervention decisions that are *consistent* over time. The adjustment of CCM interventions over time also stems from the improvement of the accuracy on customer knowledge.

There are a few technical issues worth mentioning regarding applying the proposed framework to real business problems.

First, each of the components of the framework needs to be modified to make it more practical. For example, the number of future periods that a company should consider depends on the nature of the business environment and the company's goal. Suppose the average customer tenure is three years, then the company may only need to look at a three-year period or less in its CLV objective. The real-time learning can also be more practically defined as daily, monthly, or quarterly.

Second, the rapid updates of customer information leads to an "explosion" in the number of states and control variables. This problem hinders estimation and is appropriately called the "curse of dimensionality." However, heuristic methods may still allow implementation of such an approach. The interpolation methods developed by Keane and Wolpin (1994) are a good example.

Third, even companies that cannot implement the proposed framework will find it useful to conceptually frame their marketing problems in this way and derive some heuristic rules that capture the key features of optimal solutions. For example, from the proposed framework, if we can derive some statistical properties that describe how the optimal marketing mix decisions are driven by important customer- or company- specific variables, and we can use the values of these variables to implement heuristic decisions that mimic the optimal ones.

Last but not least, the amount of data collection, standardization, and integration efforts needed at a practical level to implement the CCM framework is not insignificant. Thus, a useful way to approach the implementation of these methods is to begin with a pilot that demonstrates the effectiveness and only then move toward an enterprise-level deployment.

How Is Customer-Centric Marketing Advancing Current Marketing Practice?

First, most existing data mining tools focus on understanding customer preferences or predicting customer decisions, which corresponds to the customer response model and heterogeneity ingredients of our framework. However, our integrated framework goes beyond learning about customer response. It explicitly derives a sequence of customized and dynamic marketing decisions that cultivate the relationship with the customer over time and maximizes the total long-term profit contribution of all customers. It is, therefore, more closely related to management science than data mining. The resulting decisions can be automated in real time using software.

Second, we segment customers based on their sensitivity to marketing mix variables rather than on static demographic characteristics and the like. Only then do we profile customer segments based on demographics. This is in contrast to the current practice of segmenting customers based on observed demographics, ignoring the heterogeneous effectiveness of marketing mix efforts. In other words, rather than segment customers by their age or income brackets, we advocate segmenting them according to how sensitive they are to promotions such as coupons. Once we identify distinct segments in terms of reactivity to promotions, we can then look for proxies in the demographic features of a particular segment for easy heuristic identification. For example, the coupon-sensitive segment may be characterized by predominantly young, lower income bracket customers. The main point is that the coupon sensitivity defines the segment definition rather than the demographic profiling that was later used to proxy for it. These econometrically driven segments are more instructive and appropriate for CCM rather than static segmentation. By learning and acting upon detailed, transactional data, firms can actually find much more interesting segments than by lumping them into demographic groups.

Third, most of the existing CLV analysis calculates the net present value of customers' future profits, and treats this value as another segmentation variable in designing targeting strategies. In contrast, we treat the company as a forward-looking decision maker, which takes into account the long-term profit implications of customer attrition when making a current decision. The future consequences in terms of both revenue and marketing profit are built into the derived optimal decisions.

Fourth, most current practice[3] takes an ad hoc approach to segmentation leading to ad hoc inferences. However, we formulate the idea of segmentation in which customer information is accrued continuously and integrated into the company's periodic decisions.

Fifth, our framework integrates learning and acting upon customer information. Customer response close on the heels of a firm's marketing treatment is treated as input for the firm to update its beliefs on the customer in the next period. The optimal marketing decision is thus adapted to the most updated knowledge the firm has on the customer. More precisely, we should term the two steps as "adaptive" learning and "proactive" acting upon customer information (more details will be described in chapter 7). This is different from the data mining tools and marketing decision support tools that go through separate paths in current practice.

Sixth, the integrated framework allows the company to experiment with alternative strategies. This speeds up the learning of individual customer preference, making it possible for the decision support algorithm to be improved continuously.

Seventh, the proposed framework helps the firm reap the value of detailed customer information on their purchase history. For building long-term relationship with a customer, detailed information on each individual customer such as purchase history is more important than the size of the sample. Detailed customer information is different and complements the value of big data.

Outline of the Book

We can also now explain how the four ingredients, which are described in the next four chapters, are essential to the above model.

The customer choice models capture the basic utility function of various products offered to the customer. These specific customer choice models can be used in various models of revenue, ranging from simple retention in a plan to a choice of one of several options in a multitiered pricing plan or even the choice of products that are cross-sold by the firm. Such models are discussed in chapter 3 on customer choice models.

Chapter 4 discusses various forms of customer segmentation in which the utility functions of customers are classified into "latent classes." Each class signifies a different sensitivity in the utility function to parameters such as promotion, price, and quality. This can then be extended to be a static function of the demographic characteristics of a customer such as age or income.

Chapter 5 discusses the core elements of the CLV model that uses the customer choice functions to capture revenue and also consumption functions over time to determine varying costs of servicing customers in the future. This chapter also discusses how the CLV objective generates forward-looking profits in the firm's optimization problem.

Chapter 6 discusses some approaches to solving the dynamic optimization problem. In particular, it shows how a simple, dynamic programming approach can be used to solve the problem in all but the most complex case.

Chapter 7 describes continuous learning and adaptive decision making. It uses the interactions with customers over time to let the firm continuously improve the precision of its knowledge of customer segment memberships. This way, an adaptive learning loop is set up in the firm's optimization problem, which is superior to a static learning or segmentation solution.

Chapter 8 closes the discussion by presenting managerial implications of adapting such a strategy both in the short and long term.

Illustrative Examples: From Concept to Reality

We choose four particular cases to demonstrate the ideas and value of the proactive CCM framework and its four modeling ingredients. We call them (1) bucket-pricing of service plans, (2) win-back strategies, (3) cross-selling campaigns, and (4) allocation of service calls. Readers are invited to consult the references from which the illustrations below are drawn for more details.[4]

Case 1: Bucket Pricing of Service Plans

The Challenge   When they sign up for a service plan, cell phone customers choose an option from a pricing "bucket." The options vary from low-priced plans that come with a limited number of minutes to high-priced plans that come with thousands of minutes. Each plan has its own restrictions and allowances. On the surface, this seems like a customer-centric way of offering value. But, since consumers have difficulty predicting their usage level, the cell phone carrier benefits. The benefit comes from penalizing customers on both counts of excessive and moderate usage. This is a pain point for customers, and a source of "churn" in the industry.[5]

With the proliferation of tiered-pricing schemes (such as cable services, cell phone calling, and data plans) in the services sector, firms have been able to infer customer choice behavior across plans more carefully by analyzing vast amounts of historical data on individual transactions in their IT systems. How can the firm segment customers into appropriate plans? How can it increase the proportion of customers in more profitable plans?

In our application, we look at an online DVD rental service with several plans, each with a different quota of consumption. The objective is to determine the optimal pricing for these plans using the available data.

Problem Formulation   Here is a list of issues to be considered when building the four modeling ingredients.

1. Customer response models

   • What should be the customer choice set? How do customers make service plan choice decisions?

   • How do customers predict future consumption needs?

   • How are customer plan choices affected by price and quota, which are the two salient features of bucket pricing?

- Do customers consider stock-out or over-purchase, both of which measure the difference between consumption needs and the purchased quota?
- How would you take into account the cost of plan switching?

2. Heterogeneity

- Do customers differ in their sensitivity to price, quota, stock-out and over-purchase?
- How many segments of customers exist, and how do they differ in demographic details?

3. CLV

- How much profit can a customer contribute to the company over the customer's lifetime (taking into account the customer's plan switching decisions in the future)?

4. Dynamic optimization

- How should a firm determine the optimal monthly fee and quota that maximizes its total profit?

Note that the problem could also be more simply treated as a static optimization problem as the fee and quota are less likely to change over time.

The Solution It is well known, for instance, that customers subscribing to a plan with a much higher quota than their usage tend to deviate to lower quota plans or leave the service altogether. Our CCM based model takes such switching behavior into account in capturing CLVs and uses it to find optimal prices for each plan.

Our customer plan choice model recognizes the price structure and the role played by the instantaneous quota (which restricts consumption amount at the daily level). It also accounts for customers' switching costs and over-purchase. The model allows customers to form expectations of their future consumption needs, which encapsulates the elements of the customer's dynamic decision process like uncertainty about consumption needs, and expected stock-outs.

Applying the model to the data, we find that in choosing a plan with a larger quota, the benefits (of reducing the risk of stock-out for the current period in the short run and facilitating learning in the long run) are weighed against the costs (of higher payment in the short run and lock-in in the long run) in the customers' decision calculus.

Based on the parameter estimates obtained in the customer response model, we treat the problem of setting prices of service plans as the firm's optimization problem and conduct counterfactuals that explore the impact of the company's alternative pricing strategies.

The Results   Sample alternative designs from a pricing optimization procedure are outlined in table 2.1 along with improvements in the total profit from a sample data set.

Case 2: Win-Back Strategies

The Problem   Customer churn has become an important parameter in measuring the success of service marketing. Firms try to win back customers who have either left them or are on the verge of doing so. As companies accumulate more customer information, it is easier to predict if and when a customer is prone to defect to a competitor.

We formulate the company's decisions of *what to offer* and *when to offer* the win-back plan with a CCM model that captures the customers' evolving needs and preferences (e.g., price and service quality).[6] We use the data from the earlier example of the DVD rental firm to model a customer's chance of defecting from the firm. We consider the possibility of offering a menu of rescuing plans. The objective is to retain such customers, and use the data about past customer behavior to determine when to offer this retention plan and to whom it should be offered.

Problem Formulation   Here is a list of issues to be considered when building the four modeling ingredients.

1. Customer response models
   - What should be the customer choice set?
   - How do customers predict future consumption needs?
   - How are customer retention decisions affected by price and quota, stockout, or over-purchase (the difference between consumption needs and quota)?
   - How about service quality (especially given online DVD rental was a new service in early 2000s when this case is set)?
2. Heterogeneity
   - Do customers differ in their sensitivity to price, over purchase and service quality?

Table 2.1
Alternative product design under bucket pricing

Plan	Defection	1	2	3	4	5	6	Total revenue	Total cost	Total profit
Current design								$199K	$59K	$140K
Quota	0	1	1	2	3	5	7			
Current price	$0.0	$9.95	$12.95	$19.95	$27.95	$37.95	$57.95			
Purchase share	19.3%	0.85%	2.75%	69.1%	5.12%	2.85%	0.10%			
Usage share	0.00%	0.43%	1.48%	82.1%	8.77%	6.71%	0.50%			
First-best design								$244K	$69K	$175K
Quota	0	1	2	3	4	6	10			
Best price	$0.0	$14.6	$16.9	$30.5	$38.2	$44.1	$55.4			
Purchase share	23.3%	1.87%	2.99%	66.2%	0.62%	3.08%	1.96%			
Usage share	0.00%	0.70%	2.40%	88.6%	1.04%	6.24%	5.38%			
Second-best design								$241K	$69K	$172K
Quota	0	1	2	3	5	6	10			
Best price	$0.0	$11.2	$20.7	$22.9	$31.8	$36.5	$56.4			
Purchase share	23.7%	2.53%	1.96%	67.5%	1.31%	1.89%	1.09%			
Usage share	0.00%	0.70%	2.00%	90.3%	0.52%	3.10%	3.36%			

Source: Sun, Li, and Sun 2015b

3. CLV
   - How much profit can a customer contribute to the company over the customer's lifetime (taking into account the customer's plan to leave in the future)?
4. Dynamic optimization
   - The company has three types of rescuing plans to offer: decreasing monthly fee, increasing quota, and improving the service quality.
   - Solve for the optimal rescuing decision (when to offer which rescuing plan to which customer) that maximizes the total profit.

Note this problem could be treated as a dynamic optimization problem.

The Solution   We use a binary choice model to capture the customers' evolving needs and preferences. We then formulate the company's decisions of *what to offer* and *when to offer the rescuing plan* as optimal solutions to a dynamic optimization problem.[7]

This approach resulted in an 11 percent higher expected profit than the prevailing practice based on the data collected.

The Results

Box 2.1
A Sample Output of Win-Back Decision

Customer ID: 123456

Gender: Male

Education: College

Results of Customer Knowledge

   Possible reason for leaving: Under-usage of purchased quota

   Expected lifetime profit: $123

Recommended Decision Resulting from "Proactive" CCM Framework

   Action: Offer discount with lower quota

Case 3: Cross-Selling Campaigns
The Problem   Despite the increasing investment in cross-selling efforts, companies find that million-dollar marketing campaigns often fail to generate

revenue or even cover the cost of the campaign. Improving the effectiveness of cross-selling campaign in a cost efficient way is a major challenge for cross-selling firms. Managers face many questions: How do we tailor a cross-selling campaign to the changing needs and preferences of a customer? How do we improve the average response rate of a cross-selling campaign?

In order to address these questions, it is important to understand the role of a cross-selling campaign, how it interacts with the development of customer demand, and the trade-off between short-term campaign costs and long-term profit gains.

We look at the example of a national bank that offers a variety of products and services with cross-selling potential.

Problem Formulation Here is a list of issues to be considered when building the four modeling ingredients.

1. Customer response models

   - What should be the customer choice set?

   - What role does the bank's cross-selling effort play?

   - How are customer decisions on opening new accounts affected by cross-selling?

   - What other factors are likely to affect customer purchase decisions?

   - Do customer preferences for different financial products evolve over time?

2. Heterogeneity

   - Do customers differ in their sensitivity to cross-selling campaigns?

3. CLV

   - How much profit can a customer contribute to the company over the customer's lifetime (taking into account the customer's plan to leave in the future)?

4. Dynamic optimization

   - The bank decides when to cross-sell a specific financial product—to a specific customer—using a specific communication channel.

   - Solve for the optimal cross-selling decision (when to cross-sell which financial product to which customer using which communication channel) that maximizes the total profit.

Note this problem could be treated as dynamic optimization problem. Dynamic segmentation can be incorporated.

The Solution   We first develop a multivariate customer-response model in order to capture the possibility that customer demand for various financial products is governed by evolving financial states.[8] Customers have different preference priorities as well as responsiveness to cross-selling solicitations for different financial products. We capture long-term effects of solicitations of cross-selling in changing the speed of customer movement along the financial maturity continuum. We provide for cumulative effects on purchase probabilities.[9]

On calibrating our model to customer purchase histories provided by the national bank, we find that customer responsiveness to solicitations change when they move along a financial continuum over time. They start with products that provide financial convenience, move to those that provide financial flexibility, and then to those that potentially offer higher returns. We find that, in addition to generating instantaneous purchases, cross-selling solicitations educate customers and build goodwill in the long-run. We also find that customers have differential preferences for email or snail mail communication channels that vary across latent financial maturity states. Emails are clearly more effective in educating customers.

Based on the estimated customer-response parameters, we formulate the firm's cross-selling decisions as solutions to a stochastic dynamic programming problem that maximizes customer long-term profit contribution. The proposed dynamic optimization framework allows us to integrate intra-customer heterogeneity and the long-term dynamic role of cross-selling solicitations from the customer response model. It results in a sequence of solicitations that represent an integrated multistep, multisegment, and multichannel cross-selling campaign process about *when* to target *which* customer with *what* product using what preferred campaign channel (*how*).

The Results   We demonstrate that the effectiveness of a cross-selling campaign improved from 5.6 percent to 11.2 percent. We also calculate the indirect educational effect of a cross-selling campaign to be 63 percent. We show that the ROI of a cross-selling campaign has improved by 40.8 percent and demonstrate an increase in long-term profit when the company shifts its cross-selling strategy from campaign-centric to customer-centric.[10]

Comparing our results with several alternative cross-selling approaches in which intra-customer heterogeneity and/or educational roles are ignored and in which the cross-selling decisions are made in a myopic way, the proposed dynamic programming approach improves immediate response rate, long-term response rate, and customer long-term profit contribution (e.g., by 56 percent, 149 percent, and 177 percent over the observed data, respectively).

Box 2.2
A Sample Output of Cross-Selling Campaign

Customer ID: 654321

Gender: Female

Education: College

Current Ownership: Checking, saving, money market

Previous Cross-Selling Contacts: Email six times, telephone call five times

Results of Customer Knowledge from "Adaptive" Learning

    Financial maturity: Stage 3 (investment and risk covering)

    Duration in current financial state: 13 months

    Estimated months to switch state: 5 months

    Channel preference: Email

	Email	Telephone
Expected probability of immediate response	0.23	0.11
Expected cost for this campaign	$0.57	$1.54
Expected lifetime profit	$1,000	$900

Recommended Decision Resulting from "Proactive" CCM Framework

    Next product to introduce: Life insurance, brokerage, annuity (in the order of purchase likelihood)

    When to contact: (1) Educational campaigns within the next three months followed by (2) promotional campaigns

    How to contact: Email or direct mail

Case 4: Allocation of Service Calls

The Problem With the development of off-shore call centers, many firms are apprehensive about placing a key CCM asset in the hands of a third-party provider. At the same time, they are also keen on leveraging the strength of offshore centers to improve the service effectiveness without incurring significant costs. This requires the company to develop a CCM algorithm that allows for learning about the heterogeneous preference of customers (in terms of service duration and sensitivity to being served offshore) as well as the comparative advantage of call centers, calculates the trade-off between operating efficiency and marketing effectiveness, and allocates customers to call centers according to their sensitivities.

Problem Formulation   Here is a list of issues to be considered when building the four modeling ingredients.

1. Customer response models
   - What should be the customer choice set?
   - How are customer retention decisions affected by their experience with offshore centers (or the company's decision to route them to offshore centers)?
   - What other factors are likely to affect customer retention decisions?
2. Heterogeneity
   - Do customers differ in their sensitivity to being served by offshore centers? Can the company revise their belief about customer sensitivity to offshore centers based on the last customer-company interaction?
3. CLV
   - How much profit can a customer contribute to the company over the customer's lifetime (taking into account the customer's plan to leave in the future)?
4. Dynamic optimization
   - The company decides on which center to allocate the customer.
   - Determine the optimal service allocation decision that maximizes the total profit.

Note this problem could be treated as dynamic optimization problem. Adaptive learning can be incorporated.

The Solution   We treat service duration as a measure of operation efficiency, as well as a determinant of customer retention or marketing effectiveness. The company's optimal allocation decision is formulated as a dynamic control problem in which the firm does the following: (1) recognizes customer-specific service costs and the long-term marketing consequences; (2) learns about customers' heterogeneous preferences on service allocation; (3) balances the trade-offs between short-term service costs and long-term customer reactions; and (4) makes optimal allocation decisions that best match customer preferences and maximize long-term profit.

On the basis of estimated parameters, we conducted simulations and applied our framework to derive the optimal call-allocation decisions. We demonstrate that adaptive learning allows the firm to improve its allocation decisions by matching customers with their preferred service centers. The results show that by recognizing customer aspects, and taking into account customer retention and CLV, our proposed model reduces attrition rate significantly and also improves profit.

The Results Compared with the currently adopted "skill-based" routing (i.e., routing the customer to the agent with the lowest average service duration), the optimal allocation decisions derived from our framework (1) improve customer retention by 8 percent; (2) reduce average service costs by 6 percent; and (3) enhance total profits by 15 percent because of the growing relationships.

Thus, service effectiveness can be improved without incurring a significant cost. The proposed solution is different from conventional ways of improving customer retention by incurring more costs to increase service quality.[11]

Box 2.3
A Sample Output of Call Allocation Decisions

Customer ID: 56789

Gender: Male

Education: Graduate School

Type of Call-in Question: Software installation

Results of Customer Knowledge from "Adaptive" Learning

   Customer Type: Handholding customer who prefers longer service duration

	Onshore	Offshore
Expected service duration for this call	14 min.	12 min.
Expected probability of retention after this call	0.75	0.72
Expected service cost for this call	$11	$7
Expected lifetime profit	$297	$341

Recommended Decision Resulting from "Proactive" CCM Framework

   Action: Allocate to offshore center

In figure 2.1 and boxes 2.1, 2.2, and 2.3, we used sample data to demonstrate how the customer knowledge obtained from adaptive learning and the optimal CCM action can be translated into customer scoring and to recommend interventions. Take the service allocation as an example. When a service department receives a call, the customer's background information is traced and shown on the operator's screen. The results of this particular adaptive learning algorithm show that this customer is a "hand-holding" customer who prefers longer service duration. Given this updated information on customer type, the expected service durations and probability of retention are calculated using the customer response models of duration and retention. The total profit is also calculated as the CLV similarly defined by the equation. Comparing the total profit of onshore and offshore routing, offshore routing is recommended as the company's action.

Summary

In this chapter, we have discussed the two-step procedure (learning and acting upon customer information) and three decision components for CCM: *learning* (of customer individual preference), *forward-looking* (into future marketing consequences of current CCM interventions), and *dynamic optimization* (to optimally balance cost and benefit). We then formulate CCM interventions as solutions to a stochastic dynamic programming problem under demand uncertainty in which the company learns about the evolution of customer demand as well as the dynamic effect of its marketing interventions, and makes optimal CCM decisions to balance the cost of interventions with the long-term payoff. The framework allows us to integrate all the inter- and state-dependent factors that drive the CCM decisions. It leads to an inter-temporally related path that is consistent with the objectives of CCM. We have shown four examples that demonstrate the input, output, and benefit of CCM. The proposed solution enables companies to find real-time solutions to their marketing problems using customer data that is rapidly becoming available.

Skills to Master

- *Identify the four ingredients of CCM: choice modeling, segmentation, CLV modeling, and adaptive learning.*
- *Formulate the given marketing problem in an optimization framework to reflect learning about customer choices and forward-looking orientation by the firm.*
- *Understand the features of the resulting CCM solutions.*
- *Understand how the framework has been applied to a variety of substantive marketing problems including bucket pricing, win-back strategies, cross-selling strategies, and service allocation methods.*

3 Modeling Consumer Choice

Key Ideas

- The logit model is used to formalize discrete customer choices. The model becomes progressively more relevant as more individual customer level information becomes available.

- Depending on the nature of the predicted variables, there are binary, multinomial, and multivariate logit models.

- The estimated coefficients in the regression models measure the effect of the explanatory variables on the dependent variables.

- You can use most standard statistical software such as R, SAS, SPSS, and STATA or libraries in Python to estimate logit models. However, we present a way to do this from scratch in this chapter for better understanding.

Motivation

The logit model has now become a standard tool for estimating the impact of the variables of a marketing mix on consumer choice. The model has been extensively applied in marketing to scan data collected from panels of households and also to estimate market shares. The popularity of the model can be attributed to the ease of its application and reliability of its results. Researchers using the logit model focus, typically, on consumer responses to the pricing and promotional decisions of a firm.

In this chapter, we explain the basic ideas of consumer choice models, the first ingredient of the CCM framework. Consumer choice models allow us to set up a utility function for a typical customer and use it to predict the probability of (1) continuing a service with the firm, (2) choosing one of several pricing plans, or (3) subscribing to more than one service. Such discrete choice models can then be incorporated in the calculation of the expected future revenues from the consumer that then feed the CLV expression.

The workhorse of computing discrete choice model parameters is called maximum likelihood estimation (MLE). It is also the method that underlies regression analysis. To keep our treatment comprehensive, we first introduce a binary choice model (binary logit), and outline the basic steps to compute the optimal parameters by using the MLE method. We then extend it to multiple and mutually exclusive choice models (multinomial logit) and to general multiple-choice models (multivariate logit). We give a short illustration for each of these cases with an example of how the MLE method is set up from scratch in a spreadsheet and how it can be used to estimate the optimal parameters. The chapter concludes with a couple of exercises on the applications of these methods.

Binary Logit Choice Model

The logit choice model has been popular in marketing research. It has been particularly useful in situations where the dependent variables are binary, for example, whether or not a consumer makes a purchase, and whether or not a consumer stays with a firm.

Consider the case of a consumer who is subscribing to a service that she consumes at varying rates over several periods of time. Some examples would be cell phone plans (with minute utilizations) and Internet plans (with data utilizations). Suppose we also have the possibility of a marketing action (such as a price discount for the coming month) that can be performed on the consumer. We could model the process of customer retention as a function of both her current consumption in the plan and of the impact of the marketing action on her decision to stay on for the coming month.

This is a particularly simple case where we assume that the consumer i's decision to retain the service at time t, denoted as $RET_{it} = 1$, is based only on two parameters, namely, the level of service she is consuming and the marketing promotion she is considering. $RET_{it} = 0$ if she is not retained at time t—namely, if she does not continue with the service at time $t + 1$.

How can we model the probability of customer retention? Using a standard practice in choice models,[1] we use a random utility model of consumer choice as follows: at time t, for a given consumer i with consumption C_{it} and given the binary action variable A_{it} (set to 1 if the marketing action is performed on the consumer at that time, and 0 otherwise), we formulate the linear utility function U_{it} for the consumer as follows:

$$U_{it} = b_0 A_{it} + b_1 C_{it} + b_2 + \varepsilon_{it}$$

We assume a linear combination of the firm's action and consumption in the utility function at this particular period. Depending on the context and the relationship between customer choice and explanatory variables, other functional forms can be adopted as the utility function. For example, a squared term or a log term of consumption can be included. The coefficients b_0, b_1 are sensitivity parameters for each of the independent variables affecting the utility. They are positive if an increase in the variable causes utility for the consumer, and negative if it causes disutility for the consumer. If b_0 is estimated to be positive, it means the action taken by the firm (such as a promotion) has been effective in terms of retaining the customer. Similarly, a positive b_1 means that the customer appreciates the consumption of the service. In such a case, the higher the consumption, the more likely she is going to stay with the service provider. The term b_2 captures the customer's intrinsic tendency to stay. The last term, ε_{it}, is a random utility term that is drawn from a distribution. It varies from one consumer to the other, and models idiosyncrasies across individual choices. This random term is typically assumed to be independent across customers and time.

Choice models involve picking the one that gives higher utility. They also involve comparisons between customer retention and cancellation. Since the utilities are in arbitrary units, we can normalize one of them (say, when the customer cancels) to have the value $0 + \varepsilon'_{it}$, where the error term models his random utility if he does not have the service. The consumer stays with the service (or is retained) whenever the difference in utility between staying and canceling is strictly positive. Note that this in turn depends on whether $b_0 A_{it} + b_1 C_{it} + b_2 + \varepsilon_{it} > \varepsilon'_{it}$. This can be rephrased as whether or not the $\varepsilon'_{it} - \varepsilon_{it}$ term is at most the sum of the first three utility terms.

Two common assumptions about the distribution of the ε terms lead to two natural choice models. If it is assumed to be distributed normally, we get the class of probit models.[2] On the other hand, if it is assumed to be distributed according to an extreme value distribution (also called the log Weibull), then we get the logit model that we will be working with. In the latter case, the difference of two such extreme value random variables is distributed according to the logistic function (with cdf $F(x) = \dfrac{e^x}{1 + e^x}$), which gives the model its name.

Thus, in the logit model, we have

$$P(RET_{it} = 1) = P(\varepsilon_{it} - \varepsilon'_{it} > -(b_0 A_{it} + b_1 C_{it} + b_2)) = P(\varepsilon'_{it} - \varepsilon_{it} < (b_0 A_{it} + b_1 C_{it} + b_2)).$$

Here the last equality follows by symmetry of the logistic function around zero.

From the definition of the cdf (cumulative distribution function) of the logistic function, this is exactly given by the following expression:

$$P(RET_{it} = 1) = \frac{e^{b_0 A_{it} + b_1 C_{it} + b_2}}{1 + e^{b_0 A_{it} + b_1 C_{it} + b_2}}$$

This is the probability of customer retention. The probability of leaving the service provider is then given by

$$P(RET_{it} = 0) = 1 - P(RET_{it} = 1) = \frac{1}{1 + e^{b_0 A_{it} + b_1 C_{it} + b_2}}$$

The estimation results from logit and probit models are extremely similar (since their cdf's are very similar), particularly when the probit function is scaled so that its slope at $y = 0$ matches the slope of the logit.

Maximum Likelihood Estimation

The MLE method for determining the values of the coefficients b_0, b_1, b_2 is a simple optimization method to arrive at the most likely or plausible values for these coefficients. It is based on the principle of treating them as variables and seeking to set them to values so as to maximize the likelihood of seeing the data.[3] For this, we first need to set up an expression for the total likelihood of seeing the given data as a function of the unknown coefficients b_0, b_1, b_2 and then solve for the values of these parameters that maximize this likelihood. We illustrate this in the following example.

Given a panel of customer data that captures their retention behavior, how can we set up the problem of estimating the parameters in the choice model?

In table 3.1, we see the information for five customers; the first was retained in the second, third and fourth periods. She left at the end of the fourth period and drops out of the sample in the fifth period—thus her total tenure is four periods, and the second column records the total tenure of the current customer. The third column records whether the customer is retained for the next period and hence is derived from the previous column. For example, customer 3 was

Table 3.1
Customer retention panel data sample

Customer	Time	Retention	Action	C
1	1	1	1	1.400842
1	2	1	0	5.405517
1	3	1	1	12.71471
1	4	0	0	21.03207
2	1	0	1	1.509191
3	1	1	1	1.498887
3	2	0	0	4.481748
4	1	1	1	1.259986
4	2	0	0	4.28707
5	1	1	1	2.135138
5	2	0	0	8.110898

retained in period 1 but not retained in period 2. The fourth column records the marketing action A performed by the firm on customer i in a particular period t (it was 1 in the first and third periods for the first customer), while the final column gives the consumption C during the period for the corresponding customer.

We can now use the data to set up an expression for the likelihood of the retention decision seen so far, assuming that each row of the panel is independent of the other. Consider the first row with values $A = 1$ and $C = 1.40$. This customer has indeed retained the service for the second period so we have $RET_{it} = 1$. For a given fixed estimate of the coefficients b_0, b_1, b_2, the probability of this happening is

$$p_{1,1} = P(RET_{1,1} = 1) = \frac{e^{b_0 1 + b_1 1.4 + b_2}}{1 + e^{b_0 1 + b_1 1.4 + b_2}}$$

Similarly for the second row, we have the first customer retaining service again giving

$$p_{1,2} = P(RET_{1,2} = 1) = \frac{e^{b_0 0 + b_1 5.4 + b_2}}{1 + e^{b_0 0 + b_1 5.4 + b_2}}$$

Note that we have updated the value of the action and consumption variables to correspond to the values in this row. We compute the probability $p_{1,2}$ to be that of the actual retention action for this row, which is $RET_{1,2} = 1$.

Continuing in this manner, the fourth row is now

$$p_{1,4} = P(RET_{1,4} = 0) = \frac{1}{1 + e^{b_0 0 + b_1 21.03 + b_2}}$$

Note again that we have computed as $p_{1,4}$, the probability of the actual retention event that took place, which is that the first customer did not retain the service and hence $RET_{1,4} = 0$. We then move to the second customer in the fifth row and get

$$p_{2,1} = P(RET_{2,1} = 0) = \frac{1}{1 + e^{b_0 1 + b_1 1.51 + b_2}}$$

Having computed the values $p_{1,1}, p_{1,2}, \ldots, p_{5,2}$ across table 3.1 in this way, we can now set up the expression for the total likelihood function, assuming that these probabilities are independent.

$$L = \prod_{i=1}^{5} \prod_{t}^{T_i} p_{it}$$

Here, T_i is the total number of observation periods for customer i. Maximizing this likelihood is equivalent to maximizing the log of this value, giving the following log-likelihood function that is easier to work with, in practice:

$$LL = \sum_{t=1}^{5} \sum_{t}^{T_i} \log p_{it}$$

Note that since each of the p_{it} terms is a function of the coefficients, so is the log-likelihood function LL. Hence, the coefficient estimation problem is the simple optimization problem of varying the parameters b_0, b_1, b_2 to maximize LL. It is easy to set up the likelihood values p_{it} and their logarithms along the corresponding rows of the spreadsheet that contains the above panel data, and add them to get the function LL.

Finally, using the Solver program available as an add-in in Excel (or any other optimization solver), one can choose values for the changing cells containing b_0, b_1, b_2 so as to maximize the value of the LL cell. The shell spreadsheet with instructions titled BLEShell.xlsx[4] sets up the corresponding MLE problem, and the filled version BLE.xlsx contains the solution after running Solver.[5] The final values of the parameters are also shown in figure 3.1.

G	H	I	J	K	L	M	N
b_0	b_1	b_2					
2.574966376	0.088315	-1.24812					
			Prop 1's	0.814978		Likelihood ratio index	
MLE:		-32.8203	Rest. MLE	-47.2146		LRI	0.30487
			MLE: Max above sum of log likelihoods by varying b_0, b_1, b_2,				

Figure 3.1
Final parameter values for the example after running Solver to maximize the log likelihood.

Goodness of Fit

Classical regression models have R^2 values readily available from the estimation. Linear regression models construct a goodness-of-fit measure for estimating the coefficients. A relatively simple proxy for the familiar R^2 statistic in the case of logistic regression is the likelihood ratio index (LRI), which is defined as follows:

$$LRI = 1 - \ln L / \ln L_0$$

The term $\ln L$ represents the log likelihood of the observed data with the best estimated parameters (the best value of LL above), while $\ln L_0$ represents the same when the estimation is carried out only for the constant term (i.e., setting each of the coefficients except the constant one to be zero); the latter is called the restricted log likelihood. The best value for this constant term can be calculated using basic calculus and its formula is given below, where n is the number of observations in the data and P is the proportion of observations where the predicted dependent variable is one.

$$\ln L_0 = n[P \ln P + (1 - P) \ln (1 - P)]$$

The filled sheet BLE.xlsx contains a calculation of the LRI for the computed optimum coefficients. Note, however, there is no natural interpretation of the LRI as for the R^2 except that the index ranges from 0 (for the case when the model with only the constant coefficient is the optimal model) to values approaching 1 (as the weighted combination of explanatory variables do a better job of explaining the outcome). It is exactly 1 when a single input dummy variable is perfectly correlated with the outcome and hence the utility function with a very large coefficient for this dummy variable and no constant coefficient can very accurately predict the output.[6]

Why Solve from Scratch?

The reader may be wondering why we have gone through the laborious process of estimating these consumer parameters from scratch, especially given the variety of software packages available for data analysis.

The reason is threefold. First, it allows the reader to appreciate the reasoning that underlies the consumer choice models by implementing the ideas in the spreadsheet shell. Second, this grounding is essential when we try to generalize these models to not only include more choices but extend them to latent class segmentation for which plug-and-play software packages are not so readily available. Finally, even if all of these estimations were computable in a standalone package, the final task of integrating the inferred values in the eventual CLV model must be done deliberately and explicitly in our model. That is why we use the spreadsheet shells to build these ideas from the get go.

Multinomial Logit Choice (MNL) Model

How can the framework we developed above for binary choices be extended to situations involving more than two choices, for example, when customers choose one among K mutually exclusive plans with an additional option of defecting to a competitor in each period, giving a total of $K + 1$ alternatives? MNL models are used in applications in marketing that have several distinct outcomes. One common application is to predict what product or brand a customer is going to choose. Another application is to predict an outcome when the consumer may have more than two options, for example, pay a loan installment, pay off and close the loan, or default.

The MNL model is similar to the binary logit model, except that the dependent variable will have multiple discrete outcomes, instead of just two. The estimation technique is very similar to the binary logit model, except that instead of predicting the odds of 1 vs. 0, it predicts the odds of the different outcomes vs. a baseline outcome. For example, for a model with three outcomes A, B, C, it estimates odds of B vs. A and C vs. A.

The generalization is immediate where we postulate a different set of coefficients b_{0j}, b_{1j}, b_{2j} for each choice j and combine them in the natural way as follows:

$$P(Decision_{it} = j) = \frac{e^{b_{0j}A_{ijt}+b_{1j}C_{ijt}+b_{2j}}}{\sum_j e^{b_{0j}A_{ijt}+b_{1j}C_{ijt}+b_{2j}}}$$

In particular, the random utility derived from choice j is represented by the term $b_{0j}A_{ijt} + b_{1j}C_{ijt} + b_{2j}$ along with a random utility term that is customer specific or idiosyncratic. Note that the independent variables take on different values for the different choices available. For example, the marketing action may be undertaken for choices A and C but not for B thus giving us different values for the independent variable corresponding to action for each of the three choices. Thus, it is important to note that we allow the coefficients to be choice specific. As before, we can normalize the deterministic part of the utility function for one baseline option to be zero, simplifying one of the expressions in the denominator to one. The rest of the estimation proceeds as before; one of the exercises gives a context for extending the binary logit model to the multinomial setting.[7]

Multivariate Logit Choice (MVL) Model

How about situations where not only more than one choice is available but the customer makes each choice based on the same underlying set of independent variables? For example, a customer is sent promotions involving cross-sold products with a bank, and she makes the choice of trying out each of the products based on the same set of variables, such as her account balance, her methods of banking and her frequency of operating current accounts. We can now model each of the binary decision variables using a binary logit model. But we must be mindful that the variables across the various models are shared.

The simplest case for estimating these various decision coefficients in the logit model is when we assume that the error terms in each of these different logistic functions for each of these choices are independent of each other. We simply multiply the probability of each of the choices as though they are from different customers. We then proceed in the same way as we did for the binary logit model in estimating the parameters for the various choices.

The more involved cases of multivariate logit models assume *interaction* across various choices made by the same customer. One simple way to model this is to convert the setting to a MNL model by having one option for each outcome of the set of choices (for example, if the customer is considering adopting a checking or a savings account, there are four possibilities in the enumeration: no adoption, adoption of checking only, adoption of savings only and adoption of both. If there are three choices each with three options, then the number of exhaustive options already explodes to 3^3 or 27). Now each of these options is included in an MNL model where the coefficients are estimated separately for each option. While this exhaustive method works, it results in very large models and hence has very large data requirements.

An intermediate heuristic is to use only those combinations that are realistic among the set of all combinations in the MNL reformulation. Another option is to use more advanced statistical packages that can compute dependent estimations across various choices by using either correlation estimations, or a method of simultaneous equations. In these more advanced approaches, one can capture earlier choices in the determination of the utility for later choices (for example, when having a checking account is a precursor for opening an investment account).

The multinomial logit model is different from the multivariate logit model. Note that multinomial logit typically refers to models with a *single dependent variable* of more than two categorical values. In multivariate logit, by contrast, there are *multiple dependent variables* and it is a collection of multiple logit models. Each logit model could be binary or multinomial as defined before. There are other related models, such as the nested logit model, which can be applied to a situation where one set of decision variables is conditional on (or nested within) another set of decision variables. For example, customers make their choice of annual health insurance at the beginning of each calendar year. Then, conditional on the chosen insurance plan, they make consumption decisions (on whether to see a doctor or get a medical treatment) all through the year, before they are allowed to switch insurance plans.[8]

Augmenting the Utility Function

For demonstration purpose, we used the simplest functional forms for the consumer choice model. In reality, we need to incorporate all the explanatory variables that drive consumer choice and consumption behavior that usually vary with the context. As a rule of thumb, we recommend three groups of variables be included. The first group includes the constant terms that capture consumer intrinsic preference for choice and consumption, which usually vary with choices. The second group includes the firm's actions such as price, promotion, sales channels, service interventions, etc. The coefficients of firm actions reveal the effectiveness of firm's actions on consumer choices. They are important feeders to our dynamic programming problem as the control variables that affect customer lifetime value.

The third group of variables includes consumer-specific time dependent variables that explain consumer decision rules. There variables are usually dependent on the past (and hence encode a lagged effect) and are made available in longitudinal data. The coefficients of these variables reveal consumer preference in a turbulent market environment. For example, it is well established in the marketing literature that consumers either develop inertia or seek variety over time. That is, they are likely or unlikely to purchase the same subsets of brand repeatedly because of familiarity, learning, or decreasing loyalty. A simple way to capture this phenomenon is to include a lagged brand choice dummy indicating which brand this consumer purchased in the last or a recent period of time. If the coefficient of this variable is estimated to be positive, it signals inertia. Otherwise, consumers demonstrate variety seeking behavior. Similarly, in some applications, reference prices may play an important role. We can include the price paid last time as a way to account for the possibility that this price has any effect on the current choice. Alternatively, we can include gain and loss defined as the difference between the current price and the past paid price and let the data tell us how the perceived gain and loss affect consumer choice decisions.

When deciding on which variables to be included as explanatory variables, we encourage readers to think beyond the list of variables that are available in the data-capture system. The right way to start is to put oneself in a consumer's mindset, try to imagine the economic and psychological thinking processes that consumers follow, and create new list of variables to approximate these processes. The marketing literature has documented a number of interesting time-varying consumer specific behavioral variables that play important roles in consumer decision process in various context such as switching cost, learning of product quality and reduction of uncertainty, brand loyalty, addiction (related to consumption), and the distance to the reward threshold in a loyalty program (the coefficient reveals whether there is a point pressure effect). It is helpful to consult the marketing literature for such hints on important variables to be included for different product categories and purchase contexts.

It is important to include these variables as the coefficients of these variables offer insights on consumer decision process that cannot be studied using cross-sectional data (or big data without longitudinal information). These are the key variables for the firm to understand how each individual consumer evolves over time, predict his or her action in the next period and hence can make a customized and dynamic marketing action that is relevant to his or her stage of development.

Skills to Master

- *Know when to apply the logit model and understand the differences between binary, multinomial and multivariate logit models.*
- *Understand the principle behind maximum likelihood or know how to use appropriate software to estimate a logit model.*
- *Know how to interpret the coefficients and evaluate their statistical significance.*
- *Know how to develop the utility function so as to include all the variables that describe the dynamic customer decision process that leads to the observed choice sequence.*

Exercises

1. Facespace is a new paid social networking service for which a customer signs up and pays a monthly fee. Data collected from the firm is provided in the attached sheet "Chapter3-Ex1.xlsx" (see note 4).

The consumption pattern (in minutes) has been recorded for analysis by the system per month (under the column named C) and also indexed by customer ID (first column). The second column labeled "tenure" records the number of past months the customer has been with Facespace. The Action column records a binary digit, indicating whether the customer was offered a marketing action in the form of discount coupons with affiliated shopping sites in that month. The Retain column records whether the customer was retained for the next month. The last four variables are demographic in nature: W encodes the gender of the user, X denotes the number of children, and Y is a score provided by a partner site on a certain activity level of the customer in the web. (Only those with values above 2 were solicited to join Facespace). Finally, Z denotes the fraction of time the customer spent in shopping sites affiliated with Facespace when logged into the network.

Assume that customers i's utility in period t, U_{it}, is a linear function dependent on the variables A_{it}, C_{it}, W_i, X_{it}, and Y_{it}

$$U_{it} = b_0 A_{it} + b_1 C_{it} + b_2 W_i + b_3 X_{it} + b_4 Y_{it} + b_5$$

Here, the b's are the parameters to be estimated. Assume also that customer retention behavior is modeled by a logistic function of their utility, so the probability that customer i retains in period t, is $e^{U_{it}} / (1 + e^{U_{it}})$

Let's model this a bit more explicitly.

i. Write an expression for the likelihood function

$$P(RET_{it} = 0 \mid A_{it} = a, \ C_{it} = c, \ W_i = w, \ X_{it} = x, \ Y_{it} = y)$$

ii. Look at customer number 10 in the data set, who is present for two periods. Suppose

$$b_0 = 2, \ b_1 = 0.1, \ b_2 = -0.5, \ b_3 = b_4 = 0.3, \ b_5 = -1,$$

and assume that the retention decisions in the two observations are independent. Compute the probability of observing that retention behavior (over two periods) conditional on the values of the variables A, C, W, X, and Y in these two periods; that is, compute

$$P(RET_{10,1} = 1 \ \& \ RET_{10,2} = 0 \mid A_{10,1} = 1, \ A_{10,2} = 0, \ C_{10,1} = 3.91, \ C_{10,2} = 18.91,$$
$$W_{10} = 1, \ X_{10,1} = X_{10,2} = 1, \ Y_{10,1} = 2.85, \ Y_{10,2} = 2.07)$$

iii. Assuming all observations are independent, how would you compute the joint likelihood of observing the retention decisions in the given data, conditional on the given observations of the A, C, W, X, and Y variables? You can briefly describe how you would do this in Excel (no need to give an expression).

In the maximum likelihood estimation of the b_i's, we seek to maximize this joint likelihood. Since this value is typically very small, we work with maximizing the logarithm of the joint likelihood. Run this maximum likelihood estimation for the retention decision, based on the logit model described above and report the values of the coefficients.

2. (Multinomial logit regression) In this exercise, the cell-phone plan choices made by a group of customers over time are recorded (see Chapter3-Ex2.xls). In the worksheet, records are indexed by customer ID (cust_id) and tenure. In each period, a customer is offered two cell-phone plans, where she can purchase one, or decide not to purchase. Each plan is described by a quota-price pair (P_j and Q_j) for choice plans $j = 1$ and 2, where the customer pays the price and can use the service for up to the quota (in number of hours). The quota data are stored in columns Q1 and Q2, while price data are stored in columns P1 and P2.

We use a random utility model for each customer's purchase decision. We assume that the utility of consumer i purchasing plan j at time t is

$$U_{ijt} = b_0 + b_1 Q_{ijt} + b_2 P_{ijt} + b_3 X_i, \ j = 1, 2$$

In the equation, X denotes the number of children. The utility of no-purchase is normalized to zero. The probability of consumer i purchasing plan j at time t follows the multinomial-logit formation:

$$\Pr(CHOICE_{it} = j) = \exp(U_{ijt}) \bigg/ \left(\sum_{j'=1}^{2} \exp(U_{ij't}) + 1 \right)$$

Assuming all observations are independent, how would you compute the joint likelihood of observing the choice decisions in the given data, conditional on the given observations of X, Q_1, Q_2, P_1, and P_2? Run the maximum likelihood estimation for the choice decision and report the values of the coefficients.

3. (Multivariate logit regression) In this exercise, the decisions on whether to open a checking account, a savings account, or both, made by a group of customers, are recorded (see Chapter3-Ex3.xls). In the worksheet, each record corresponds to a customer. The first two columns record consumer decisions on opening checking and savings accounts, where 1 means an account is opened by the customer. The column X records the number of children of the customer, and the column Y records a centered measure of the past usage frequency of banking services of the customers obtained from an external source.

There are two steps in this exercise. In the first step, we treat the decision on the checking account as independent from that on the savings account. Each decision involves the use of a binary logit model, where the utility is

$$U_{ijt}^c = b_0^c + b_1^c X_{ijt} + b_2^c Y_{it}$$

$$U_{ijt}^s = b_0^s + b_1^s X_{ijt} + b_2^s Y_{it}$$

Estimate the above two models separately and report the results.

In the second step, we treat these two decisions as made jointly. That is, a customer is choosing from four options simultaneously: both checking and savings accounts, checking account only, savings accounts only, and neither. This is represented as a multinomial problem, where the utility functions are

$$\begin{cases} U_{ijt}^c = b_0^c + b_1^c X_{ijt} + b_2^c Y_{it} \\ U_{ijt}^s = b_0^s + b_1^s X_{ijt} + b_2^s Y_{it} \\ U_{ijt}^{cs} = b_0^{cs} + (b_1^c + b_1^s) X_{ijt} + (b_2^c + b_2^s) Y_{it} \end{cases}$$

Notice that the utility function shows that the benefit (or cost) attributable to the number of children and past consumption are additive between checking and savings accounts. However, the constant term for opening both accounts is not necessarily the sum of the two individual constant terms. This is to take into account any possible complementary or substitution effects between the two services.

Estimate this multinomial logit model. Compare the result with the previous step, and comment.

4. Instruction for analyzing data in the four cases for models of customer choice: Examine the data provided with each of the four cases described in chapter 2. This is the first of three sets of exercises in which you will work with that data to apply the models you learned to build elements of the customer centric models for these cases. For each of the cases answer the following questions:

   a. What is the set of choices available to the customer?

   b. What statistical method will you use to model the customer's future choices?

   c. What are the explanatory (independent) variables in the model?

   d. What do you expect will be the sign of the coefficient for each of the explanatory variables in your model and why?

   e. Are any of your explanatory variables redundant (containing the same or very similar information as another)?

   f. Are your explanatory variables exhaustive (not missing effects that are important)? If not, can you add any derived variables or dummy variables?

   g. Should you consider changing the functional form of any of these variables (like taking the log or square of the variable) to highlight any suspected effect?

   h. More generally, consider other customer-related variables that you would like to learn about, for example, the customer's future "consumption" of the product or the service offered by your firm. How will you model the trend of this variable?

   i. Should you be considering the multinomial or multivariate extensions of the choice models in modeling the customer choices?

Examples

First Direct Makes Informed Marketing Decisions

First Direct[9] is an Internet bank in the United Kingdom. It was among the first to break, in the late 1980s, the traditional mold of brick-and-mortar and branch-based banking. It has arguably the world's most loyal banking customers by effectively deploying one of the most satisfying service interfaces in the financial services sector. The bank developed a new kind of employee in the banking system, called the "banking representative" (BR), to deal with customers exclusively over the phone. BRs were mostly women, who were taking a few years off from their careers as lawyers, accountants, and business managers, to care for children, and who wanted jobs with flexible hours. They had never worked in any of the banks, but came with what First Direct recognized as "life skills."

Each BR was provided with a workstation that could access the bank's customer information systems at three levels: customers' identity data (name, address, phone number, age, and income); how they came to the bank; and when they opened their account. They also tracked histories of customer accounts, such as deposits, withdrawals, transfers, changes of job or address, and past purchases of banking products or services. Customer call representatives in most banks viewed such histories as transactional. BRs viewed them as behavioral. They gleaned insight into customers' future needs and desires. The system was soon self-perpetuating. It accumulated emotional data, such as a BR's observations of a customer's moods, personality, and disposition, which enabled other BRs to interact with the callers according to each customer's preferences and individual style. The system was refined to a degree that it signaled to the BR, at the start of each call from a returning customer, not only what to discuss but also how to discuss it.

By the early 1990s, First Direct had achieved customer satisfaction rates above 90 per cent and nearly perfect levels of account retention. It went on to qualify at the top of the UK banking industry's customer satisfaction rankings for twelve years (and counting), starting in 1991. When accounts were closed, it tended to be for one of two reasons: either the account holder was moving out of the United Kingdom (the bank's only market) or that person had died.

The bank has since developed new concepts like First Direct Lab, where customers are encouraged to come up with innovative ideas that First Direct could use to develop and deliver new products and services.

Entravision Relies on Technology to Process Data Speedily

Entravision[10] is a Spanish language broadcasting company in the United States focused on Hispanics as its core segment. It set up a subsidiary in 2012 called Luminar to manage its customer information. As the first step, Luminar built a database of US adults (numbering 140 million) and a subset of Hispanic adults in the United States (numbering 37 million). These were part of what was known as structured data, culled largely from electoral rolls. It then went on to mine "unstructured" data, as in social media tools like blogs, tweets, and YouTube. Together, it generated, on a preliminary reckoning, about 125 terabytes of living, breathing data for analysis in real time.

As part of the second step, it ingested all the data into an open source platform with a capacity to process 140 million adult records in forty-eight hours. The platform consisted of a central processing unit and a parallel cluster of low-cost commodity servers, each containing a local disk to hold a subset of data. Luminar deployed an algorithmic approach, known as MapReduce, to perform four sequential processes: "reading" the data from the disk, "mapping" the data by applying a variety of filters, "reducing" the data by summarizing it in specified ways, and "writing" results back to the disk. The algorithm cut processing times dramatically. It took a conventional platform six hours to process one petabyte of data. MapReduce did that in thirty minutes.

Luminar was able to append the right records and the right transactions (particularly the ones below the radar) to the right consumers and, by extension, to the right households. By identifying specific consumption patterns, it was able to build unique consumer profiles. The profiles were based, not on self-reporting as in a focus group or an opinion poll, but on what, why, and how people were consuming at the grassroots. The resulting data helped the legion of advertisers of Entravision make informed choices in targeting customers for their product promotions.

4 Segmenting Customers into Latent Classes Based on Sensitivity

---

Key Ideas

- Consumers can be segmented based on their sensitivities to the marketing mix variables. We call this "unobserved consumer heterogeneity." This is different from the more popular approach that classifies consumers based on observable customer features like demographics.
- Unobserved segments can be automatically identified as differing sensitivities to different parameters in the customer's utility function.
- The probability of belonging to each segment will be estimated together with a choice model that automatically classifies customers.
- The probability of segment membership can be specified as a function of observed demographic variables (both static and time-varying).

In this chapter, we extend our discussion of consumer choice models by introducing the idea of segmenting customers based on the probability of their choices such as retention of a service. This probability is linked to parameters that influence customer retention, such as consumption and marketing intervention as in the last chapter. The key distinction of our particular segmentation is that it is not based on any observable static characteristics, such as demographic data or past consumption. It is based on *unobservable* characteristics of the customer, which are her sensitivities to factors that determine the utility function. Our segmentation procedure uncovers what are typically termed in the marketing literature as *latent classes*.[1]

Traditional Classification Approach

Traditional models of segmentation rely on static and observable profile values. They classify customers according to demographic profiles in order to target them for different types of marketing actions.

Indeed, a lot of current analytical advances in marketing involve clustering models in which the information collected about customers are regrouped to arrive at specific profiles. In one extreme, only static data about customers, such as their age, gender, and address is used. At the other extreme, the set of data collected in the interaction with the customer is captured in a high-dimensional vector. In either case, the data are fed to a classification method such as decision tree induction, association rule mining, market basket analysis, or any of several clustering methods[2] to determine inherent segments in the customer profiles. The resulting segments are then analyzed and labeled carefully to identify their key features. Marketing decisions (such as targeted intervention or channel selection) are taken by matching each decision optimally with the features of the corresponding segment. Young customers, for example, may be sent email, while others may be sent regular mail for promotions.

It is important to note that this is *not* the kind of segmentation we advocate in this book. While static segmentation has been extremely useful in the past, it is not clear if it corresponds to variations in customer reactions over time. Moreover, since the traditional approach uses estimates of a customer's retention and consumption choice model parameters, any error in estimation will percolate into proactive marketing decisions using static segments making the latter less effective.

Our solution to this shortcoming is to use the data to automatically predict the segments in the customers. In particular, we assume there are inherent and unobservable segments among customers and that each segment corresponds to customers with very different utility (and hence response) functions affecting their decision. We then use the observed customer retention data to determine these segments automatically. Once we develop the conceptual framework, doing the estimation of the coefficients for these segments from the data reduces to an exercise in estimating the segment parameters. We do this next with an example.

Two Latent Classes in a Binary Logit Choice Model

Consider again the case of a consumer whose retention probability for a service depends only on a marketing action (such as a price discount for a coming period). We can use the method in the previous chapter to model the consumer's decision to retain the service based only on a single parameter of whether he got the price discount for the period.

As before, we would assume a linear utility function for customer i in period t, for retaining the service:

$$U_{it} = b_0 A_{it} + b_1 + \varepsilon_{it}$$

Here the coefficient b_0 is the sensitivity parameter for the action term A_{it} and b_1 is the intercept capturing the intrinsic utility for this customer from the service. Recall that in the binary logit model, we assume that the ε_{it} term is a random utility term drawn from an extreme value distribution, giving us the following expressions for the probability of retention:

$$P(RET_{it} = 1) = \frac{e^{b_0 A_{it} + b_1}}{(1 + e^{b_0 A_{it} + b_1})}$$

$$P(RET_{it} = 0) = \frac{1}{(1 + e^{b_0 A_{it} + b_1})}$$

The simplest model introducing two latent classes of customers assumes that each customer comes from one of two distinct classes. Thus, customers from Class 1 will have sensitivity parameter and intercept terms b_0^1 and b_1^1 respectively, while those from Class 2 will have the same being b_0^2 and b_1^2.

To model the presence of two latent classes of customers, as above, we postulate a probability that the customer is from class 1, $q_1 = P(Seg_i = 1)$, and the remaining probability that he is from the second, $q_2 = 1 - P(Seg_i = 1) = 1 - q_1$. Then the probability of an arbitrary customer being retained can be worked out as follows.[3]

$$P(RET_{it} = 1) = P(RET_{it} = 1 \ \& \ Seg_i = 1) + P(RET_{it} = 1 \ \& \ Seg_i = 2)$$

Expanding using the definition of conditional probabilities and noting $q_1 = P(Seg = 1)$, we get[4]

$$P(RET_{it} = 1) = q_1 P(RET_{it} = 1 | Seg_i = 1) + q_2 P(RET_{it} = 1 | Seg_i = 2)$$

If we now use the different parameters in the Logistic retention function for the two different classes, we have the following expression for the probability of retention of a typical customer:

$$P(RET_{it} = 1) = q_1 \frac{e^{b_0^1 A_{it} + b_1^1}}{(1 + e^{b_0^1 A_{it} + b_1^1})} + q_2 \frac{e^{b_0^2 A_{it} + b_1^2}}{(1 + e^{b_0^2 A_{it} + b_1^2})}$$

Using the same line of reasoning we get a similar expression for the probability of no retention of a typical customer:

$$P(RET_{it} = 0) = q_1 \frac{1}{(1 + e^{b_0^1 A_{it} + b_1^1})} + q_2 \frac{1}{(1 + e^{b_0^2 A_{it} + b_1^2})}$$

We now have the main ingredient to use the MLE method to try and estimate the b-parameters, noting that we have one more additional parameter ($q_1 = P(Seg_i = 1)$) also to estimate. Another important feature of the estimation procedure is that it takes care of dependencies in the time-series of interaction with a single customer. We address that next.

Maximum Likelihood Estimation of Latent Classes

The main challenge in extending the MLE method, which we saw in the previous chapter, to the case of latent class estimation, is to incorporate the dependencies in the data rows we get from the same customer.

Here is a typical snapshot of the time-series data from two customers from a larger panel.

Cust-id	New-cust?	Tenure	Action	Retain?
1	1	1	1	0
1	0	2	1	0
1	0	3	1	1
1	0	4	1	1
1	0	5	1	1
1	0	6	0	0
1	0	7	1	1
1	0	8	1	1
1	0	9	1	1
1	0	10	1	1

Cust-id	New-cust?	Tenure	Action	Retain?
2	1	1	0	1
2	0	2	1	1
2	0	3	0	1
2	0	4	1	1
2	0	5	1	1
2	0	6	1	0
2	0	7	0	0
2	0	8	1	1
2	0	9	1	1
2	0	10	1	1

The first column is the ID of the customer. For each customer, we have ten rows of data despite the fact that we have not retained the customer over the whole ten time periods. The second column now has a flag (1) whenever the rows start the time series for a new customer. The third column indexes the tenure of data recorded for the current customer. The fourth and fifth columns indicate whether the marketing action was performed during that period and if the customer was retained at the end of that period (for the next time period). For example, the first customer was given the marketing action in all but the sixth time period. Nevertheless, he was not retained in the first, second and sixth periods. This implies that he was a customer of the firm only during periods 1, 4, 5, 6, 8, 9, 10, and 11, and was not retained in periods 2, 3, and 7. Note that the non-retention in period 7 follows the lack of a marketing action in period 6 indicating a potential correlation. The next ten rows give similar data for the second customer.

In the original MLE method (with a single latent class), we considered each row corresponding to different interactions with the same customer (such as the first ten rows) to be independent observations. Consequently, in the objective, we simply included the product of the observed outcomes (labeled p_1, p_2, p_3, etc., in the previous chapter) as the likelihood to be maximized. However, this method is not sound when we have two classes and we consider the different observations from the same customer. In particular, we need to model the case where the customer 1 is either in segment 1 (with probability q_1) and all her ten observations of retention (or non-retention) were based on this assumption, or that she is in segment 2 and her observations are conditioned on this latter assumption. Thus, the term for the likelihood for customer 1's observations in the MLE objective is as follows:

$$p(1) = P(Seg_1 = 1 \, \& \, Cust1 \, Data) + P(Seg_1 = 2 \, \& \, Cust1 \, Data)$$
$$= q_1 \left(p_1^1 \cdot p_2^1 \cdots p_{10}^1 \right) + q_2 \left(p_1^2 \cdot p_2^2 \cdots p_{10}^2 \right)$$

Note as before that since the first customer had $RET_{1,1} = 0$ in the first step,

$$p_1^1 = \frac{1}{(1 + e^{b_0^1 A_{1,1} + b_1^1})}$$

Similarly, since he had $RET_{1,3} = 1$ in the third step, we have

$$p_3^2 = \frac{e^{b_0^2 A_{1,3} + b_1^2}}{(1 + e^{b_0^2 A_{1,3} + b_1^2})}$$

Note how we have changed the sensitivity parameters (b's) depending on the segment that we assume the customer to be from.

Now the final MLE objective function is just the product of the objectives over all the observed customers:

$$L = \prod_{\text{customers } i} p(i)$$

Using Equal-Length Panels from Customers

We now point to another important requirement of the panel data we use in the latent class estimation. Suppose we have time series data where we have only five observations from customer 1 and ten observations from customer 2. Building the single customer's likelihood estimate $p(1)$ from the product of the probabilities of her five observations, while doing the same for $p(2)$ from ten observations, causes an imbalance in the contribution of these values to the final MLE estimate. In particular, the first customer has a much larger estimate contribution (product of five probabilities) to the objective than the second (product of ten probabilities). Hence, her data will have a much higher influence in determining the solved values for the sensitivity estimates (and the segment probabilities) than that of customer 2, even though ironically, we have more data for the second customer.

This example serves to illustrate the care that one must take in using latent class choice models: when we use time-series panels from customers to estimate segments, we must ensure that all panels we use in the estimation are of the same length (same number of time periods) to give equal representation to every customer's data in the estimation. We must ensure that less available data does not weigh in more on the outcome than others. Luckily, modern CRM systems capture a continuous time-series of interactions with customers. Even if the interactions are not current, the objective is to win the customers back. They provide a time series of the same length for most active customers. Even otherwise, the data from CRM systems can be truncated (in terms of going back in time) up to a point where sufficient data is available to carry out the latent class estimation analysis.

Putting It All Together

As with the usual MLE estimation method for the binary logit model in the last chapter, we can now finish the estimation procedure after recalling and using some modeling tips. We transform the product of likelihoods to a sum of log-likelihoods as before:

$$LL = \sum_{\text{customers } i} \log p(i)$$

Note that in this case, the $p(i)$'s are a function of the coefficients from two different classes as well as the probability q_1, and so is the log-likelihood function LL. Hence, the coefficient estimation problem is the simple optimization problem of varying the five parameters $b_0^1, b_1^1, b_0^2, b_1^2$, and q_1 to maximize LL. We need to set up constraints in the optimization problem to keep the value of q_1 in the range [0,1] but this turns the estimation method into a nonlinear problem with constraints, which is not very well-behaved.

A useful trick in the case with only two latent classes is to use the transformation $q_1 = 1/(1 + \exp(\lambda))$. Here λ is an unconstrained real number which is then used as the (unconstrained) variable in place of the original (constrained) variable q_1, leading finally to an optimization problem over five unconstrained variables $b_0^1, b_1^1, b_0^2, b_1^2$, and λ.

As before, it is now routine to set up the cumulative likelihood values $p(i)$ for each customer i and their logarithms along the corresponding rows of the spreadsheet that contain the panel data, and add them up to get the function LL. Finally, using the Excel Solver program, one can choose values for the changing cells containing $b_0^1, b_1^1, b_0^2, b_1^2$, and λ so as to maximize the value of the LL cell. The enclosed LC-BLEShell.xlsx spreadsheet sets up the corresponding MLE problem. The filled version LC-BLE.xlsx contains the solution after running Solver.

Determining Latent Class Membership

The solved version LC-BLE.xlsx also contains a column that illustrates a simple example of Bayesian update used to determine which of the two segments each customer is from. This column is titled *Revised P(Seg = 1)* and denotes the current belief probability that the customer is from segment 1. We initialize this after the first observation from each customer based on the prior probabilities that the estimation determined. In particular, the initial estimate for this probability is q_1 so the first observation updates this to the revised value $q_1' = p_1^1 q_1 / (p_1^1 q_1 + p_1^2 q_2)$. The formula implements a simple conditional probability definition: the denominator gives the total likelihood of the current customer's observations consisting of the two parts corresponding to the customer coming from segment 1 and from segment 2. The numerator contains only the likelihood containing the term corresponding to the customer coming from segment 1; the ratio thus reflects the revised probability of the customer coming from segment 1. This logic can be repeated as more observations cumulate by using the revised value of segment membership from before, and using the cumulative probability of all the observations seen so far for this customer.

In the next step we continue updating, but our current estimate for the probability that this customer is from segment 1 is q_1'. The cumulative probability that this customer is from segment 1 after two updates is the product $p_1^1 \cdot p_2^1$, while the same for segment 2 after these two updates is the product $p_1^2 \cdot p_2^2$. Thus, the revised probability that customer 1 is from segment 1 after two observations is now

$$q_1'' = \frac{p_1^1 \cdot p_2^1 q_1'}{p_1^1 \cdot p_2^1 q_1' + p_1^2 \cdot p_2^2 (1 - q_1')}$$

Since we have a cell in the spreadsheet tracking the cumulative probability under the assumption that the current customer is from segment 1 (call it $Pcum_1$), and a similar probability for segment 2, we can use these in the generic updates as follows:

$$q_1^{rev} = Pcum_1 q_1^{old} / (Pcum_1 q_1^{old} + Pcum_2 (1 - q_1^{old}))$$

Note how these revised values converge toward 1 or 0 (denoting increased confidence of the customer in segments 1 or 2 respectively) as we increase the number of observations, showing evidence of learning of the customer segment.

Joint Estimation of Latent Class Properties

In anticipation of our application of these latent class estimations, we note that when we posit two customer segments and also estimate other properties about them, we need to separately identify these properties based on which segment they are from. It is similar to the case of the retention probability in the example above. Suppose we also estimate a separate satisfaction variable for every customer along with the probability of retention based on surveys from the customers that record these satisfaction values. Note that since the customers are coming from two segments, we can assume that the satisfaction values also have different sensitivities for the two customer classes. We estimate them accordingly, rather than use one set of sensitivity coefficients.

The problem becomes even more interesting if we estimate not only one output variable (such as satisfaction or probability of retention) but more than one. Even if we assume that these two variables are independent of each other, for every customer, for every segment, we first need to compute the joint probability of observing this data for both satisfaction level and retention; then we must cumulate them over all observations for this customer to get a single probability value of seeing all these observations for this customer assuming each of the possible segments. Only then can these probabilities be combined, using the probability of belonging to each segment into the overall likelihood for these observations for the customer. We will return to this nuance in the chapter on the firm's optimization problem.

Interpreting Segment Results

The estimated parameters are $b_0^1, b_1^1, b_0^2, b_1^2$, and q_1. Among these, b_0^1, b_0^2 denote the effectiveness of the firm's action on consumer retention. Similarly, b_1^1, b_1^2 represent the intrinsic preference for consumer to stay with this company for segment 1 and segment 2. Intuitively, the higher the values of b_0^1, b_0^2, the more effective is the firm's action on retaining consumers. Similarly, if b_0^1 is higher than b_0^2, it means consumers in segment 1 are more sensitive to the firm's action than those in segment 2.

When there are more variables in the utility function, we can get a better idea about how consumers differ across segments and label the segments. Accordingly, suppose that consumers in segment 1 have a larger coefficient on price and promotion and a lower coefficient on a variable denoting search cost. Then, we can label the first segment as a deal-seeking segment and the other segment as a convenience-seeking segment, depending on the research context.

At an individual level, q_1 is the probability of belonging to the first segment and $1 - q_1$ is the probability of belonging to the second segment. At the aggregate level, it can also be interpreted as the proportion of consumers belonging to the first segment.

Linking Segment Membership with Consumer Demographics

We can make the segment probabilities (q_1 and q_2) functions of other customer variables. In a simple variant, which is also reminiscent of regular clustering methods alluded to in the beginning of this chapter, we can make the probability of being in segment 1 a simple function of some demographic variable, say D, available with the customer profile. This can be accomplished by changing to functional form for the probability of belonging to segment 1 as follows:

$$q_1 = 1 / (1 + e^{\lambda_1 D + \lambda_0})$$

Here we make both λ_0 and λ_1 unconstrained variables, thus introducing one more parameter in the estimation than before. The variable λ_1 represents how the demographic variable D affects the probability of a consumer belonging to segment 1.

For example, a positive λ_1 can be interpreted as follows: the higher the income (assuming D denotes income), the more likely this consumer belongs to segment 1, which could be more or less price- and promotion-sensitive than consumers from the other segment. Thus, the latent class approach advances the classification approach by not only segmenting consumers based on their sensitivities to marketing mix variables, but also by linking the segments with observed demographics.

A more sophisticated variant would be to make this probability a function of a dynamic (time-varying) variable such as the tenure of the customer with the firm or even the cumulative consumption with the firm. These can be integrated just as easily in the estimation by replacing the demographic variable D with the time-varying values, such as consumption. Such a model can capture how customers occupy one of several mature states of engagement in their interaction with a firm. Dynamic variables, such as tenure or net consumption, can capture the apparently slow but steady convergence of the customer's segment into one of these dynamic segments. An example using customer tenure as the dynamic variable is provided in the LC-BLE.xlsx spreadsheet.

Recently, sophisticated models have been developed to capture the notion that customer segment membership may evolve over time. One promising method is hidden Markov models, which not only captures the dynamics of customer relationships but also incorporates the effect of the sequence of customer-firm encounters and the subsequent buying behavior. In these models, the transitions between the states are a function of time-varying covariates such as customer-firm encounters that may have an enduring impact by shifting the customer to a different (unobservable) relationship state. The resulting model enables marketers to segment their customer base and examine methods by which the firm can alter the long-term buying behavior.

As a simple initial step, we recommend leaving the static consumer demographics in the latent class specification. The coefficients of these variables offer profile of consumers who are classified in the different segments, which is actionable for the firm. Suppose the latent class results reveal two distinctive segments: one segment has an intrinsic preference to choose brand A, is less sensitive to price and promotion, demonstrate higher brand loyalty and inertia, compared to the other segment. The coefficients of the demographic variables may reveal that older, wealthier, and highly educated consumers are more likely to belong to the first segment. Then the firm not only knows how the members in the first segment behave but also who they are approximately. Additionally, having the demographic variables in the latent class allows the model to assign individual specific likelihood of segment membership as well as the individual specific likelihood of choice and consumption for each consumer. This allows the firm to generate actions that are individual and time specific. This serves as the foundation for targeted and dynamic decision making, which is impossible if we leave out the demographic variables in the segment choice function.

Interested readers can take a look at Li, Liechty, and Montgomery (2005), Montgomery et al. (2004), Moon, Kamakura, and Ledolter (2007), Du and Kamakura (2006), and Netzer, Lattin, and Srinivasan (2008).

Skills to Master

- *Adding latent class segmentation to an existing logit model and implementing it in a spreadsheet.*
- *Interpreting the difference between segments.*
- *Incorporating demographic variables as part of segment membership propensity.*

Exercises

1. The data for this homework is in "Chapter4-Ex1.xlsx." This is a panel data
   (the observations for each customer are over 10 periods) from a banking service firm. The variables are as follows.

   a. **Customer id** is a unique identifier for each customer.

   b. **Tenure** denotes the period (between 1 and 10) when this observation is
   made.

   c. **Action** is a binary variable that is set to 1 if the bank takes some marketing
   action toward the customer.

   d. **External** is a value between 0 and 1 that captures some external market
   effects.

   e. **Retain** is a binary variable that is 1 if the customer retains his account
   with the bank for the next period. Each customer is assumed to have an
   account with the bank in his/her first period.

   The utility of any customer i in period t, U_{it} is modeled as a linear function
   on the variables A_{it} (action), and E_{it} (external), namely:

   $$U_{it} = b_0 A_{it} + b_1 E_{it} + b_2$$

   Here the b's are the parameters to be estimated. Assume also that customer
   retention behavior is modeled by a logistic function of their utility, so the probability that customer i maintains an account with the firm in period t is

   $$\frac{e^{U_{it}}}{1 + e^{U_{it}}}$$

   You believe that there are two segments of customers with different b parameters determining their utilities. In particular, there are two sets of parameters b^1
   and b^2. The utility of customers in the first segment is given by $b_0^1 A_{it} + b_1^1 E_{it} + b_2^1$,
   and the utility of customers in the second segment is $b_0^2 A_{it} + b_1^2 E_{it} + b_2^2$. Let q_1
   denote the proportion of customers in the first segment, which is also a parameter to be estimated.

   Following the example in the chapter, use maximum likelihood to estimate
   the parameters b^1, b^2 and q^1. This is latent class estimation. In the expression for
   maximum likelihood, there should be only one probability term for each customer (corresponding to ten observations).

   Run the estimation for b^1, b^2 and report the values you estimated for b^1, b^2
   and q^1.

Follow the example in the chapter to estimate the revised probability that each customer is in segment 1. Fill out a final row of your worksheet with these values as they are revised with more and more observations of the same customer.

2. Segmentation models in the cases: We will continue our case modeling by examining whether for each of the four cases, the customers in your case data set might exhibit any form of latent segmentation. In particular, answer the following questions for each of the cases.

   a. Do you expect to see natural (demographic-based or feature-based) segments among your customers? If so, what are they? What are the distinguishing features of each cluster?

   b. Consider applying the idea of latent classes among your customers. These are classes that differ in how they respond to various factors affecting their choice (such as a firm's marketing actions and other features of the product/service). Do you expect to see such latent classes in your customer data? Why or why not?

   c. If you plan to do latent class segmentation analysis of your customer, among the set of explanatory variables in your choice model, what are the relevant ones along which you expect latent class segments? Why?

Examples

AARP Segments Customers Based on Email Inactivity

AARP is a nonprofit association set up to "promote independence, dignity and purpose for older persons" aged fifty-plus. Founded in the United States, it has expanded its reach into Europe in a bid to become global in the long run. AARP has over 37 million members with whom it communicates through the medium of email. Members get discounts on a wide range of products, travel, and services in addition to lifestyle tips. They also get subscriptions for several publications of AARP.

The conventional way of segmenting a mailing list is by email activity. AARP uses email *inactivity* as the basis. The company tracks what it calls the open rate (the rate at which its emails are opened by subscribers) once in every four months. It then segments email recipients into Active (those who have opened email and took action in the last four months); Passive (those who have opened email in the last four months but did not take action); and Inactive (those who neither opened nor clicked in the last four months). Rather than write off Passive and Inactive accounts, as email marketers are prone to do, AARP makes an effort to "nurture" them in a bid to engage them once again. It treats an "engaged" email list rather than a "huge" email list as pay dirt.

AARP has been sending a series of targeted email campaigns to its Passive and Inactive segments. As a result, it has seen a 60 percent increase in its Active segment. The company is now moving to the next level by incorporating behavioral segmentation (linked to important touch points during the sales cycle) and conducting predictive modeling (targeting customers based on analytics that show what and when they would purchase next).

Wachovia Segments Customers Based on Responses to Marketing Mix

Before it was acquired by Wells Fargo in 2009, Wachovia, a diversified US financial institution at the time, had found a way to balance its short-term goal of increasing income (through tactical changes in the marketing mix) with its long-term goal of building customer equity (which it defined as the economic value derived from customers over their lifetime). It was in 2006 that Wachovia had started working on it.

The first step was the recognition that the goals were in conflict since a marketing tactic that boosted sales in the short term could have a negative effect on CLV. A systematic, data-based approach alone would help determine the total measure of return. The company started tracking marketing expenditure on three dimensions: new customer acquisition, customer retention, and customer cross-selling. It developed the database from inputs from hitherto standalone sources like the company's advertising agency (which had the historical spending allocations across media), branch network (which provided the revenue data), and the bank's Service Excellence group (which tracked customer satisfaction readings). It then factored in changes in revenue across different customer segments and also for different product categories (like deposits, credit, and investments). The impact on each element was not always symmetrical. Advertising, for example, had a stronger impact on acquisition than on retention while customer service had the reverse pattern. It was by measuring the impact on each component of customer equity and then combining them that Wachovia was able to derive the total, long-run effects of its marketing-mix decisions.

The project had led to a cultural change at Wachovia; it started looking at marketing spend as an investment rather than as a cost.

5   Customer Lifetime Value

Key Ideas

- A firm should be able to predict how its current actions affect future customer response and cost. And a firm should use that prediction to calculate CLV.
- CLV can be calculated by a simple backward table computation.
- By being forward-looking, a firm can identify trends of tomorrow and be responsible for today's actions.

We begin our discussion from the perspective of a firm that is accumulating information about customers through a CRM system. We introduce a popular measure of benefit from engaging with a customer: her CLV. It is a simple, time-discounted value of all anticipated cash flows from a customer. CLV is, in that sense, similar to net present value (NPV), a metric that is commonly used in evaluating financial projects.

CLV has been used in marketing literature as a common variable in determining both the level of engagement and the channels of engagement with customers.[1] What is new in our approach is that we show how a simple, recursive (or self-referencing) procedure can be used to compute CLV. We then use this insight to treat CLV as an objective function for a simple formulation of the firm's optimization problem in the next chapter.

The various components of CLV, such as the revenue and the costs of servicing the customer, are yardsticks in their own right, which help incorporate customer responses in the ongoing marketing decisions of a firm. They also enable the firm to be *forward-looking*. They help anticipate new streams of revenues, and thereby tweak the corresponding costs. CLV methodology can also be modified to allow *adaptive learning* to come into play. This will be the focus of our discussion in chapter 7 on adaptive learning.

Static CLV

CLV is a single number that attempts to capture the long-term value of a customer to a firm. Its definition is based on a sequence of expected future profits that are accrued from the customer at various future points of time, and is simply the time discounted value of these expected profits. If the hurdle rate per period is r, and we denote the expected profit contributed in period t by $E[PROFIT_{it}]$ for any customer i, then

$$CLV_{it} = \sum_{t'=t}^{\infty} \frac{E[PROFIT_{it'}]}{(1+r)^{t'-t}}$$

The shortcomings of this simple, static definition is that it is hard to estimate the profit from a customer in the future since it depends on choices made by the consumer both today and tomorrow. As a first step, we can convert the expected profit during a time period t into the joint probability of retention until t, $P(JRET_{it} = 1)$, multiplied by a term for the profit $PROFIT_{it}$ from this customer if he is retained. We thus get the following expression for CLV:

$$CLV_{it} = \sum_{t'=t}^{\infty} P(JRET_{it'} = 1) \cdot \frac{PROFIT_{it'}}{(1+r)^{t'-t}}$$

Profit is usually defined as the difference between revenue and cost of each individual customer at time period t. As an example, suppose the customer pays a monthly subscription fee to become a member of an online lending library and, in return, he can view either a limited or unlimited quantity of ebooks. The revenue for the firm would be the monthly membership fee and the cost could be the provision for downloading service to the particular customer.

Since both the revenue and the cost won't occur unless the customer stays with the firm, we adjust the profit by the probability of retention. This is the profit the customer contributes to the firm at time t. For period $t + 1$ and beyond, the profit will vary with time because the probability of retention will change across time.

For example, the monthly revenue could change when the firm offers multiple tiers of membership wherein the customer shifts to a higher or lower membership plan. It could also change when the number of ebooks viewed by the customer varies every month.

Table 5.1

Retention probability and profit in each period for a specific customer

Time t	0	1	2	3	4	5	6
$P(RET_{it} = 1)$	0.9	0.8	0.7	0.7	0.7	0.6	0.6
$PROFIT_{it}$	10	11	10	11	12	15	18

Thus, a forward-planning firm needs to predict both the future revenue stream and the future cost stream. In the following discussion, we first use profit to demonstrate the idea of CLV. We then separate revenue from cost.

Consider a simple example using the retention model we developed in the previous two chapters. Table 5.1 contains for each time period (including the current period labeled zero) the probability of retention of the customer for that particular period. Let us assume, for simplicity, that these probabilities of retention are independent across time periods.

Note that we can now compute the probability that a customer will be retained all the way through the tth period as follows:

$$P(P(JRET_{it} = 1) = P(RET_{i1} = 1)P(RET_{i2} = 1)...P(RET_{it} = 1).$$

Using this expression in the formula for CLV, we can evaluate it over the seven time periods given in the example above.

However, there is a simpler way to compute CLV based on the following *recursive* definition: the idea of recursion here is to make the definition of a quantity depend on a simpler version of itself.

If we let CLV_{it} represent CLV at time period t and beyond, we see that our original task was to determine CLV_{i0}. But there is a simple definition for CLV_{it}. It is based on the observation that this is exactly the sum of the profit accrued in that period t plus the expected continuation value of CLV. It can be obtained from the next period onwards, time-discounted for one period. This expected value, in turn, is the product of the probability of retention of the customer into the next time period (that we denote $P(RET_{it} = 1)$ above and in table 5.2) multiplied by the discounted CLV from the next period onwards. This can be succinctly expressed as follows:

$$CLV_{it} = PROFIT_{it} + \frac{P(RET_{it} = 1)CLV_{it+1}}{(1+r)}$$

Table 5.2
Recursive calculation of CLV for a customer

Time t	0	1	2	3	4	5	6
$P(RET_{it} = 1)$	0.9	0.8	0.7	0.7	0.7	0.6	0.6
$PROFIT_{it}$	10	11	10	11	12	15	18
CLV_{it}	...	...	...	...	$12 + 0.7\dfrac{CLV_5}{1+r}$	$15 + 0.6\dfrac{CLV_6}{1+r}$	18

Table 5.3
Recursive computation of static CLV

Time t	0	1	2	3	4	5	6
$P(RET_{it} = 1)$	0.9	0.8	0.7	0.7	0.7	0.6	0.6
$PROFIT_t$	10	11	10	11	12	15	18
CLV_t	35.81	31.55	28.26	28.69	27.79	24.82	18

Thus, we can compute CLV_{i0} by beginning with the computation of $CLV_{i6} = PROFIT_6$ and using the above formula to compute CLV_{i5} from CLV_{i6} and then CLV_{i4} from CLV_{i5} and so on. This is best done by adding a new computation row.

The computation of CLV values is thus easy to do in a spreadsheet program by adding the last row and using a particular value of r, say 10 percent. The filled values from a spreadsheet program are shown in table 5.3 giving a final CLV of 35.8, which can be looked up as the value of CLV_0 in the filled table 5.3. This is the expected time discounted value of retaining the customer for seven periods based on our retention and profit estimates.

This way of computing CLV—starting from the value in the last period and using the next period's accumulated value for the current period—is a simple example of applying backward induction to compute a recursive formula. This is also the workhorse of the dynamic programming methodology used to solve such problems.

We will use this approach in the next chapter to solve the optimization problem of deciding on the firm's marketing action to maximize CLV.

The key to using this technique is to assume that future profits are static and do not depend upon the sequence of actions performed so far. It decouples the dependencies over time and allows for values to be computed in a cumulative fashion.

Including Revenue and Consumption Trends in CLV

A simple extension to the above model incorporates the revenue and cost components. Note that we can now include information about the changing predictions of revenue expected from a customer (as we learn about her preferences for the firm's products and services) as well as the projected costs of servicing her (based on her varying consumption pattern if it is a service, and on her varying purchase behavior if it is a product). It will also incorporate any future promotional costs that might be already planned for this customer.

As an example, suppose we have a customer who has subscribed to a service (such as an Internet connection service) with a flat fee, but has varying rates of consumption. A popular and useful model for such varying consumption is to assume that its trend is log-linear. That is, the logarithm of the consumption at time t is assumed to be proportional to a linear function of the logarithm of the consumption at the previous period plus other demographic variables. For example, if the consumption at time t is denoted as C_{it}, we assume that the current time period t also denotes the total tenure of the customer with the firm. The log-linear consumption model can be expressed as follows:

$$\log C_{it} = a_0 \log C_{it-1} + a_1 t + a_2 + \varepsilon_{it}$$

Here ε_{it} is a normally distributed noise variable representing the variability associated with the specific period. Note that if a_0 is a positive value more than 1, it shows an increasing trend, while having a_1 as negative causes a dampening effect over time. We will do an example of estimating such a model in the exercises, but will focus, for now, on using such a model in expanding the *CLV* expression. To be concrete, fix $a_0 = 1.24$, $a_1 = -0.15$, and $a_2 = 0.44$, and assume that the logarithms are taken with base 10. Also assume that the fee per period charged from the customer is 5 dollars while the net cost to the firm per unit of customer consumption is 0.25 dollars. Finally, assume that the hurdle rate is 10 percent. We can now compute the *CLV* by substituting for the expected *PROFIT*$_t$ value, the difference between the fee collected in the period and the costs of servicing the expected consumption during the period.

To fill in the expected consumption, we use the trend given by the log-linear model above. We first compute the expected value of the log of the consumption and raise it to the base 10 to get the consumption values in table 5.4. The full model for computing the dynamic *CLV* is given below. The accompanying spreadsheet "Dynamic-CLVShell.xlsx" contains instructions for you to fill out this sheet, while the filled-in version is in "Dynamic-CLV.xlsx" from which table 5.4 is extracted.

We will now explain how this table 5.4 is filled out (using a spreadsheet program). Note that CLV values are not monotonic, that is, they do not always increase or decrease. They change depending upon the effect of the consumption, the retention probability and the service costs, which are inherently nonlinear.

First, we fill in the current value of the log of the consumption. Let us say the current consumption is two units; so we fill in $\log_{10} 2 = 0.3$ in the top left cell. Next, we use trend values for the log of the consumption starting with this value, updating the value for the next cell to its right with $a_0 \log C_{i0} + a_1 1 + a_2$. For the given values of the a's and with $\log C_{i0} = 0.3$, we get $\log C_{i1} = 0.66$. We continue in this way to fill out the whole row in the forward direction. Note how the log of the consumption first increases and, as the tenure increases, the dampening effect takes over and it falls even below zero by the ninth period.

The second row is obtained by simply taking ten to the power of the values in the first row to get the actual consumption values. The third row consists of given (or assumed) retention probabilities in each time step. The fourth row computes the profit at any time period by taking the fixed fee (of 5) and subtracting the variable costs of servicing the customer based on her consumption. The latter is the per-unit service cost (of 0.25) multiplied by the consumption value obtained in the second row for this period. The rest of CLV computation proceeds, as in the static case, by using the more dynamic profit values in the backward induction.

One important caveat in using the trend of expected consumption in the above calculation is that we are using expected values rather than actual "sample" values in calculating CLV. In reality, this consumer will only have these expected values of consumption in the future while the actual values will vary around these expected values. The more the variation around these values, the more inaccurate our estimation of CLV will be.

A more sophisticated approach will use the predicted trend values for the expected consumption, simulate typical sample values for a typical customer into the future, calculate CLV for each sample path and average CLV over them. The restriction of using a single spreadsheet makes such an approach of sampling and averaging beyond the scope of our presentation.

However, a lesson from this discussion is that, as the variance of the consumption process increases, the more we should guard against the use of expected

Table 5.4

CLV computation expanding profit into fee and consumption terms

Time t	0	1	2	3	4	5	6	7	8	9	10
$E[\log C_{it}]$	0.30	0.66	0.96	1.18	1.31	1.31	1.17	0.84	0.28	-0.57	-1.76
C_{it}	2.00	4.61	9.17	15.26	20.3	20.48	14.66	6.85	1.89	0.27	0.02
$P(RET_{it} = 1)$	0.98	0.95	0.95	0.95	0.90	0.90	0.90	0.88	0.88	0.85	0.85
$PROFIT_{it}$	4.50	3.85	2.71	1.19	-.07	-0.12	1.34	3.29	4.53	4.93	5.00
CLV_{it}	15.15	11.96	9.39	7.74	7.59	9.37	11.59	12.54	11.56	8.79	5.00

values and, therefore, the higher we should make the hurdle rate as a heuristic. We should also take into consideration the risk of volatile movements of the predicted consumptions from the mean values. Increased hurdle rates will guard against the risk introduced by high volatility of the consumption values in *CLV* calculation. The price we pay for this is that the computation becomes more and more myopic, putting much more weight on a few periods in the future rather than being very forward looking.

Our model for *CLV* is still rudimentary. We can make it more effective by adding the effect of the firm's actions on all the factors that affect CLV, such as the profits and the probability of retention at each time period. Since we already have a choice model, as developed in the previous two chapters, we can use that model in incorporating the consumer behavior in *CLV* computation. We will do this in the next chapter.

We notice in table 5.4 that the profit contributed by customer *i*, over time period *t*, decreases over time, and becomes negative in periods 4 and 5, before increasing over the rest of the periods. A myopic firm will give up on this customer without realizing the future profit stream from this customer. A forward-looking firm is more likely to sacrifice current profit and retain this customer in order to harvest future profit. More importantly, a forward-planning firm can carefully sequence its marketing actions in order to influence the retention and consumption pattern and hence the profit stream. Through continuous firm and customer interaction, the firm could maximize the lifetime value contributed by the customer.

This is the idea of proactively managing customer lifetime value, which will be achieved through dynamic optimization, a framework we will present in the next chapter.

Skills to Master

• *Know how to develop a spreadsheet model for calculating the static CLV using available data.*

• *Include future trends from regression models for customer consumption trends and consumer response.*

• *Understand how the firm's current action affects CLV in a forward-looking adaptation of the model.*

Table 5.5
Data for exercise 1 on static CLV

Time t	1	2	3	4	5	6	7	8	9
$P(RET_{it} = 1)$	0.90	0.95	0.85	0.75	0.90	0.50	0.60	0.80	0.60
$PROFIT_{it}$	50	100	150	50	200	100	50	200	150

Exercises

1. **Simple CLV calculation:** Table 5.5 gives data on a customer's relationship with your firm for the next ten months. The retention probability $P(RET_{it} = 1)$ in time period t equals the probability that the customer retains the firm's service for the next period (i.e., in period $t + 1$), and these probabilities are assumed to be independent across periods. The profit $PROFIT_{it}$ in period t is the money that your firm makes from the customer in that period. The customer is currently enrolled with the firm in the first period; so the lifetime value is at least \$50 (the profit in period 1). Assuming a discount factor of 0.97 from each period to the next, compute the lifetime value of this customer.

2. **Modeling consumption by the customer via a regression:** Facespace is a new, paid social networking service for which customers sign up and pay a monthly fee. Recall the data collected from the firm is provided in the attached sheet "Chapter3-Ex1.xlsx."

The consumption pattern (in minutes) has been recorded for analysis by the system per month (under the column named C) also indexed by customer id (first column). The second column labeled "tenure" records the number of past months the customer has been with Facespace. The Action column records using a binary digit whether the customer was offered a marketing action in the form of discount coupons with affiliated shopping sites in that month. The Retain column records whether the customer was retained for the next month. The last four variables are demographic in nature: W encodes the gender of the user, X denotes the number of children, Y is a score provided by a partner site on a certain activity level of the customer in the web (Only those with values above 2 were solicited to join Facespace). Finally, Z denotes the fraction of time the customer spent in shopping sites affiliated with Facespace when logged into the network.

Assume that the consumption C_{it} for any customer i in period t follows a log-normal distribution. We want to use the given data to estimate the coefficients from scratch (not using any regression package) in the following regression model:

$$\log C_{it} \sim N(a_0 \log C_{it-1} + a_1 t + a_2 Y_{it} + a_3 Z_{it} + a_4, \sigma^2)$$

where $C_{i,t-1}$ is the realized past consumption of the same customer in period $t-1$ (if this is the first period, then this value is set to 0).

Based on the least squares (OLS) estimation method from statistics, your goal is to obtain the set of a parameters that *minimizes* the sum of squared errors each of the form:

$$(a_0 \log C_{it-1} + a_1 t + a_2 Y_{it} + a_3 Z_{it} + a_4 - \log C_{it})^2$$

Do this explicitly by modeling this minimization objective function in a spreadsheet and minimizing it using an add-in such as the Excel Solver. Make sure that you start with different starting values for the alpha's to convince yourself that the solution you obtain is not a local optimum. Report the values of the coefficients (a's). These can be used as input to model the customer's evolution in the future as part of a CLV calculation.

Examples

Relay Foods Implements Promotions Based on CLV

A random survey conducted by Relay Foods, a grocery and farm product retailer focused on mid-Atlantic US markets, showed that the average basket size of customers was increasing with successive purchases. The survey was done around the time the company was set up in 2009. It became the basis for tracking the productivity of its promotional budget. The marketing spend was linked to the retention rate and future cash flows from each customer. It gradually led to the determination of the present value applied to the cash flows of customer relationship or CLV, as described above.

Relay Foods bought food products from boutique retailers, restaurants, and local farms at 15 percent lower than their in-store shelf price and delivered the goods at designated customer pickup locations at a price set at the retailer's shelf price. Its customers consisted of local residents interested in locally grown and organic foods. The company had two sets of promotions: through emails and social media; and through coupons and mailers. In a bid to attract new customers, Relay Foods offered a 10 percent discount for new customers on their second purchase and 5 percent on their third purchase. The coupons had high redemption rate at 80 percent, an indication that customers were coming back. The company was using CLV to determine three factors: profitability of promotions, how much on average a new customer would be worth in dollars, and whether customer acquisition and retention was worth the cost. The metrics were crucial to Relay Foods because it had to finance its entire operations on a budget limited by the 15 percent margin.

Bell Canada Anticipates Future Customer Calls and Takes Proactive Action

The biggest cause of excessive customer effort is the need to call back. Even if the problem that prompted the original call has been addressed the first time around, 22 percent of repeat calls invariably involve downstream issues. This is contrary to the belief of companies with strong first contact resolution (FCR) scores. Although they are well equipped to anticipate and "forward-resolve" customer issues, they rarely do so because they are focused on managing call time.

Bell Canada met this challenge by mining its customer interaction data to understand the relationships among various customer issues.[2] It began training its service representatives not only to resolve the customer's primary issue but also to anticipate and address common downstream issues. For instance, a high percentage of customers who ordered a particular feature called back for instructions on using it. The company's service representatives now give a quick tutorial to customers about the key aspects of the feature before hanging up. This sort of forward resolution enabled Bell to reduce its "calls per event" by 16 percent and its customer churn by 6 percent. For complex downstream issues that would take excessive time to address in the initial call, the company sends follow-up emails: for example, explaining how to interpret the first billing statement. Bell Canada is also weaving this issue-prediction approach into the call-routing experience for the customer.

6 Marketing Optimization Problem

Key Ideas

- CLV is refined by adding forward-looking features.
- Forecasts about customer consumption as well as their chance of retention are included in the optimization of CLV.
- Results of latent class segmentation are also used in optimizing CLV.

We extend the various components of CLV, such as revenue and marginal cost of a customer, to incorporate the response of the customer to the marketing actions of the firm. We develop this idea in stages in this chapter.

First, we look at the basic optimization problem for a firm that is facing a binary decision of whether or not to engage in a marketing action with a customer. This action carries a cost to the firm. It could also have an impact on the consumer's response in terms of her consumption and her retention over the next time period. We estimate consumption parameters, assuming log-linear consumption as in the previous chapter, to determine expected future consumption values. We then use these values, in a random linear utility function, in determining the chance of customer retention at the current and future time periods. This probability of retention thus feeds the CLV objective and introduces the vital forward-looking element in the decision-making process.

We then discuss how the optimization method can be compared with existing methods. We validate it by following an approach that is typical of data-mining applications: holding out some data and conducting, for comparison, a performance test on them with the new method.

Firm's Optimization of Marketing Action Decision

As a starting point, we consider a customer whose consumption pattern follows a simple log-linear model based on the past period's consumption and the tenure:

$$\log C_{it} = a_0 \log C_{it-1} + a_1 t + a_2 + \varepsilon_{it}$$

With ε_{it} being Gaussian distributed noise representing the specific period uncertainty, we can estimate these coefficients using OLS regression, as discussed in the previous chapter.

We also assume that the customer's probability of retention is a logistic function of a random linear utility that includes a 0–1 variable indicating if the marketing action was performed on the customer in this period and also the consumption in the current period, as introduced in chapter 3. Thus, we have the following model:

$$U_{it} = b_0 A_{it} + b_1 C_{it} + b_2 + \varepsilon'_{it}$$

Here ε'_{it} is the appropriate extreme value function giving the following expression for the retention probability:

$$P(RET_{it} = 1) = e^{b_0 A_{it} + b_1 C_{it} + b_2} / (1 + e^{b_0 A_{it} + b_1 C_{it} + b_2})$$

Again, the coefficients can be estimated from the given customer data as described in chapter 3.

The firm's optimization problem in the current time period involves a simple binary decision of setting the action variable A_{it} in the current time step t. Given the goal of maximizing CLV, the solution to this problem is to compute CLV by setting A_{it} to 0 and 1, respectively, and choosing a sequence of actions that results in the larger value.

To compute these optimal decisions, we extend the dynamic programming method to determine the optimal CLV obtainable from time t until the end of the planning horizon; let us denote this quantity by $E[PROFIT_{it}]$ for expected profit from t onward. At any time step t, this value is the maximum of the two possible choices of the action A_{it} at this time step:

$$E[PROFIT_{it}] = \max(E[PROFIT_{it}] \mid A_{it} = 0, E[PROFIT_{it}] \mid A_{it} = 1)$$

Once we fix the value of the marketing action A_{it} for this time period to 0 or 1, we can plug it into the formula for the probability of retention as above. We also need the consumption value at this time period that can be filled in by extrapolation from the current value of the customer consumption using the estimated trend function. The profit at any given step is simply a flat fee for the period minus the cost of servicing the customer (which in turn depends on the expected consumption value for the customer) minus the cost of the marketing action (if it is performed). Thus, we can now fill in the value for the expected profit when the marketing action is performed (or not) and use the appropriate formula for the probability of retention (depending on whether the action is performed or not).

In particular, let a, c, and f denote the cost of the marketing action, marginal cost per unit service, and the flat fee that is the revenue from a retained customer in one period, respectively. We have the following expression for the expected profit with and without performing the marketing action:

$$E(PROFIT_{it} \mid A_{it} = 1) = -a + f - c \cdot E(C_{it}) + P(RET_{it} = 1 \mid A_{it} = 1) \cdot \frac{E(PROFIT_{it+1})}{(1+r)}$$

$$E(PROFIT_{it} \mid A_{it} = 0) = f - c \cdot E(C_{it}) + P(RET_{it} = 1 \mid A_{it} = 0) \cdot \frac{E(PROFIT_{it+1})}{(1+r)}$$

The value of $E[PROFIT_{it}]$ is the larger of the above two. As in the previous chapter, it is best to carry out these computations in a spreadsheet starting from the last time period in the planning horizon and working backward to the first period. At the last period, the expected costs are the immediate costs. For every other period, we fill in the values for the above two expressions with and without the action, and then proceed to take the larger of the two, keeping track of the choice of the action that resulted in the maximum profit. We thus get the maximum expected profit. We can also arrive at a strategy for achieving the profit in future by following the optimal decisions encoded in the table in figure 6.3 at every period. Note that in this way, the table computation gives not only an optimal decision for the action today but also a strategy or a plan for how to continue this decision in the future to achieve the expected CLV.

As an example of the trade-off in the one stage decision problem, we have the following decision tree in figure 6.1. For this example, we assume that the expected revenue from the next period ($E[PROFIT_{it+1}]$) is $4 and the time discounting rate (r) is 10 percent, which gives a discount factor of 0.91. The marketing action has a cost (a) of $1, while the one-period fee (f) collected as revenue is $5. The unit-consumption cost (c) is $0.05, and the estimated consumption for the period ($E(C_{it})$) is ten units.

The same sheet with the formulas expanded is shown in figure 6.2.

Note that by taking into account the future expected revenues, we force the optimization decision to factor in the future consequences of the current action.

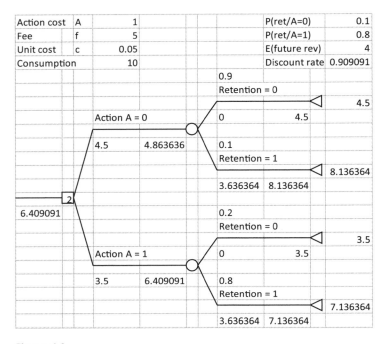

Figure 6.1
Simplified decision tree to decide on marketing action with only one period look-ahead.

In this one-stage example, the current action affects the probability that the customer will be retained in the next period. More sophisticated models can factor in more changes in future revenues in the two different scenarios, whether the current marketing action is performed or not.

Our framework allows the firm to be forward-looking, meaning the firm will be able to maximize the total profit each individual customer can contribute over her lifetime. This has at least two implications: first, the firm will realize that the current action taken by the firm has a long-term impact on the customer; in addition, the firm will be willing to sacrifice immediate current profit for future benefit from a customer. Furthermore, the firm's sequence of actions derived from our framework are inter-temporally connected. An action taken in the current period will change the course of future actions.

As a conceptual example, consider the marketing action of offering a credit card to a student. Given more and more information about her spending habits in the future (which in turn determine the expected profit for the firm), as well as the potential for fees from her in the future, a more refined value of her CLV

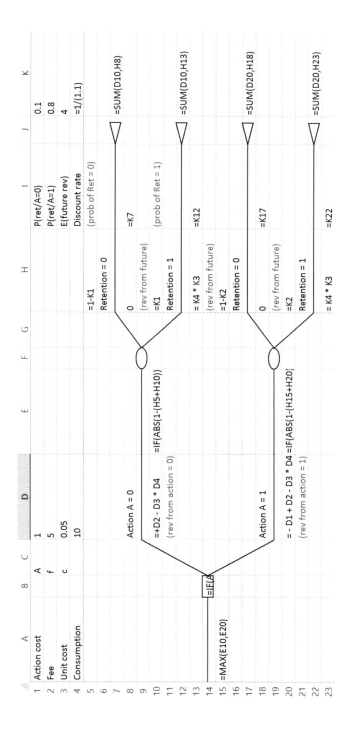

Figure 6.2

One-period decision tree with formulas exposed. Pay attention only to the formulas annotated in parentheses; other formulas using the ABS command are used to keep temporary values and can be ignored.

can be built as seen in the last chapter. However, the current action of offering her a credit card has a critical influence on this CLV; the goal is to determine the decision of offering the card based on the lifetime values that arise (or do not arise) from offering the card. Thus, if the student is confirmed to be a low credit risk with potential high spend in the future, this line of reasoning may convincingly tip the decision to offer the card.

Customized and Dynamic Action Decision

As a concrete example of the above model, consider customers signing up for an e-book rental service. They pay a monthly fee of $5.0 and the marginal cost of offering each unit of service is $0.05. The firm needs to make a decision about whether to offer a promotion of $1.0 for each customer, and if so, when to offer it. The goal is to maximize the lifetime value of each customer and hence the total long-term profit of the firm.

Suppose we run the estimation and obtain the parameters in table 6.1 for the consumption and the retention probability coefficients.

The estimates in the consumption equation imply that there is a persistent consumption pattern over time; that is, the customer forms a consumption habit over time (as indicated by the positive coefficient 1.24). Consumption of e-book usage also decreases over time (as indicated by the negative coefficient of -0.13). The coefficients in the utility function show that customers react positively to promotion (coefficient 2.57). Customers also get positive utility from consuming the e-book service (coefficient 0.09).

Table 6.1
Estimated coefficient values for log-linear consumption trends and the linear utility for the choice model that reflects the retention probability

Consumption coefficients					
a_0	a_1	a_2	Hurdle rate	Discount factor	
1.24	-0.13	0.44	10%	0.909091	
Utility coefficients					
b_0	b_1	b_2	f (periodic fee)	a (action cost)	c (unit cost)
2.57	0.09	-1.25	5	1	0.05

We can now fill in the values for the expected profit from t onward $E[PROFIT_{it}]$ in a table as we did for the CLV computation. See the spreadsheet shell "OptShell.xlsx" for a template of how this can be done. A fragment of the filled in version of the shell (entitled "OptSolutions.xlsx") is presented in the table in figure 6.3, showing also the actions resulting in the maximum expected profit at the current time. Note also how the probability of retention is higher with the action being taken, than when no action is taken. One can see a lift to the expected lifetime value that counteracts the cost of the action being performed.

Table 6.1 is filled out in a fashion similar to the CLV computation.

We begin by filling out the trend of the expected value of the log of the consumption using the coefficients we have computed in the first row. We then fill the last column for period 10 and compute the expected profit with and without the action, which is the fee minus the action, minus the cost for servicing the customer's consumption. The customer's estimated average consumption, in turn, is 10 raised to the power of the log of the consumption that has been calculated as an expected value in the first row, multiplied by the unit service cost. The utility function with and without the action being performed is similarly set up and is then used to compute the probability of retention for the next step. Finally, the maximum expected profit in the last period is the maximum of the two options with and without taking the action. This is recorded in row 2.

In the penultimate column, the calculations are similar. The expected profit calculations—with and without the action—take into account the optimum profit that can be obtained from the next period onwards along with the probability of retention and the discount rate. The revenue (flat fee), marginal costs, and action cost (if the action is performed) are also used in the computation. The optimum profit is the higher of the two options.

Once the calculation for the penultimate column is performed, it can be repeated backward to the columns before it. This is made easier by a simple copy-and-paste command in Excel that can be used to copy the values in the penultimate column to all of the previous columns (only for the second row and below).

We use this example to demonstrate a few features of the derived firm plan.

First, the output of the firm's dynamic optimization program is a *strategy* or a sequence of actions. It is a sequence of promotions for a firm to follow in order to maximize the total long-term customer value from the current period onwards.

Time t	0	1	2	3	4	5	6	7	8	9	10
E[log(C+1)]	0.30	0.68	1.03	1.32	1.56	1.73	1.80	1.76	1.59	1.24	0.67
E[opt-profit]	15.29	15.52	15.32	14.44	13.14	12.14	11.07	10.22	9.06	7.31	4.81
E[profit | A=0]	8.32	8.82	9.84	11.59	12.88	12.14	11.07	10.22	9.06	6.61	4.81
E[profit | A=1]	15.29	15.52	15.32	14.44	13.14	11.42	10.18	9.38	8.71	7.31	3.81
Utility|A=0	-1.16	-0.91	-0.38	0.56	1.94	3.45	4.35	3.87	2.13	0.21	-0.92
Utility|A=1	1.41	1.66	2.19	3.13	4.51	6.02	6.92	6.44	4.70	2.78	1.65
P[ret=1 | A=0]	0.24	0.29	0.41	0.64	0.87	0.97	0.99	0.98	0.89	0.55	0.29
P[ret=1 | A=1]	0.80	0.84	0.90	0.96	0.99	1.00	1.00	1.00	0.99	0.94	0.84
Action taken? (Yes =1)	1	1	1	1	1	0	0	0	0	1	0

Figure 6.3

Recursive computation of CLV using the estimated consumption and retention models.

Second, the promotion sequence is *customized*. It is specific at the segment level if we use the latent class approach, or at the individual level if we allow the probability of latent segment to depend on customer demographics, or if we build in adaptive learning in the firm's optimization problem (as we show in the next chapter).

Third, the solution takes into account habit formation in consumption. It recognizes each individual customer's consumption history. With all else being equal, two customers will be assigned different promotion schedules if they have a different consumption history. Following a similar logic, the dynamic nature of the solution can be enhanced if we include carryover effects such as a reference price effect, wherein customers use past prices to assess the fairness of current price. Current promotion may affect customer perception of the fairness of service offerings.

Fourth, if any changes to the customer response function results in a change to the customer's sensitivity to the firm's action (a single number) or the customer's consumption in the current period (another single number), we can see that each of these will also trigger all the numbers in the table in figure 6.3 to change.

The above demonstrates conclusively that our framework is a powerful system that takes into account not only customer current response, but also their future reaction to the firm's current action. Thus, it provides a solution to a dynamic optimization problem. The solution lies in enumerating the possible combinations of the action sequence and finding the solution that gives us the highest CLV.

Given the recursive way of computing the CLV function and our simple assumptions about the consumption trend, we have been able to solve this complicated optimization problem in a simple spreadsheet.

We can use the above example to also illustrate some key properties of optimal solution as follows. These are best followed along with the filled spreadsheet version of which we have provided a snapshot below after making *one* modification: changing the current consumption value of the customer from 2 units to 1.8 units. Note that this only affects the top left entry of the expected current consumption from $\log(2) = 0.3$ in the table in figure 6.3 to $\log(1.8) = 0.26$ in the one in figure 6.4.

However, the single change in the current consumption value changes the trend line of future consumption reflected in the row labeled $E[\log(C+1)]$. This, in turn, affects the utility function and hence the probability of retention with and without the action. Finally, these affect the overall lifetime value with and

Time t	0	1	2	3	4	5	6	7	8	9	10
E[log(C+1)]	0.26	0.63	0.96	1.24	1.45	1.59	1.63	1.56	1.33	0.92	0.28
E[opt-profit]	15.54	15.90	15.92	15.31	14.15	12.96	12.06	10.88	9.60	7.59	4.95
E[profit	A=0]	8.36	8.85	9.77	11.30	12.72	12.94	12.06	10.84	8.41	6.24	4.95
E[profit	A=1]	15.54	15.90	15.92	15.31	14.15	12.96	11.73	10.88	9.60	7.59	3.95
Utility|A=0	-1.18	-0.96	-0.53	0.21	1.22	2.18	2.54	1.90	0.58	-0.59	-1.17
Utility|A=1	1.39	1.61	2.04	2.78	3.79	4.75	5.11	4.47	3.15	1.98	1.40
P[ret=1	A=0]	0.24	0.28	0.37	0.55	0.77	0.90	0.93	0.87	0.64	0.36	0.24
P[ret=1	A=1]	0.80	0.83	0.89	0.94	0.98	0.99	0.99	0.99	0.96	0.88	0.80
Action taken? (Yes=1)	1	1	1	1	1	1	0	1	1	1	0

Figure 6.4

CLV computation by altering the initial consumption value from 2 to 1.8, reflected by changing the top left value from $\log(2) = 0.3$ to $\log(1.8) = 0.26$.

without the action leading to a different set of action choices leading to the optimal CLV.

Note that the changed consumption trend gives a higher chance of retention with the action, resulting in the action being taken in more future periods and leading to a higher CLV of $15.54 than the earlier value of $15.29.

It is now easy to use the basic model to test various other assumptions: for example, if we assume the future consumption will stay constant at 1 unit, we can change the first row labeled $E[\log(C+1)]$ to stay constant at the value of $\log(2)$ = 0.3. We then get the table in figure 6.5 calculating a revised CLV of $14.25 under these assumptions. The resulting marketing schedule advocates using the marketing action at every step.

Note that CLV calculated for a specific customer using assumptions about her consumption and other patterns yield a measure of "personalized ROI" from the marketing actions undertaken with her. In contrast with ROI measures for generic campaigns, a key benefit from these customer-centric models is a detailed view of the return on marketing spend at a very fine-grained level.

Validation of Optimization Decisions

In most cases, we can use historical data to validate the framework.[1] We can also estimate the improvement in profit dollars by assuming that all coefficients in the consumption and retention equations stay the same over time. If the lift is promising, we can then use our framework to generate action plans for future.

Let us now briefly discuss how the marketing actions advocated by our method can be tested against existing or past methods.

As is common in many data-mining studies, we hold out a fraction of the data chosen randomly for the purpose of validation, and use the remaining data to estimate the consumer behavior and retention probability coefficients. We use the held out data as test instances and apply our dynamic programming model to compute the expected CLV assuming that their consumption and retention behavior are similar to the training data we used in the estimation. By comparing the actual lifetime value obtained from these customers to the predicted values from our method, we can get a sense of the lift obtainable by our method.

A standard caveat applies. The estimated values we use in our approach may not correspond exactly to how the customer would react to our optimal set of actions. However, the expected values we compute are reasonable approximations of this number if the customer data does indeed correspond closely to the

Time t	0	1	2	3	4	5	6	7	8	9	10
E[log(C+1)]	0.30	0.30	0.30	0.30	0.30	0.30	0.30	0.30	0.30	0.30	0.30
E[opt-profit]	14.25	14.09	13.88	13.59	13.19	12.64	11.90	10.88	9.48	7.57	4.95
E[profit	A=0]	8.01	7.96	7.90	7.81	7.69	7.53	7.31	7.01	6.59	6.02	4.95
E[profit	A=1]	14.25	14.09	13.88	13.59	13.19	12.64	11.90	10.88	9.48	7.57	3.95
Utility|A=0	-1.16	-1.16	-1.16	-1.16	-1.16	-1.16	-1.16	-1.16	-1.16	-1.16	-1.16
Utility|A=1	1.41	1.41	1.41	1.41	1.41	1.41	1.41	1.41	1.41	1.41	1.41
P[ret=1	A=0]	0.24	0.24	0.24	0.24	0.24	0.24	0.24	0.24	0.24	0.24	0.24
P[ret=1	A=1]	0.80	0.80	0.80	0.80	0.80	0.80	0.80	0.80	0.80	0.80	0.80
Action taken? (Yes=1)	1	1	1	1	1	1	1	1	1	1	0

Figure 6.5

CLV computation assuming that the future consumption at every period will be the same as 1, the value in the current period. The top row is now filled with the estimate $\log(2) = 0.3$ in every cell.

models we have constructed. We can try to put confidence numbers to our esti-mates by doing goodness-of-fit tests of the predicted trends (of consumption and retention) to the actual values on the held out customer data. However, as a first cut, our validation method gives some insight into the magnitude of possible improvement.

In the "OptValdn.xlsx" spreadsheet provided, we have carried this out elabo-rately. The second spreadsheet implements the optimal strategy for held out customers by calculating the optimal expected profit for each of them along the columns of the sheet. We warn the reader that this calculation is a bit elaborate since we keep track of the *actual observed* retention pattern of the customer and use it in place of the random one assumed in the CLV calculation earlier. In particular, if the customer was retained in reality, we take the corresponding CLV value from the next step onward and use it. If not, we use the expected lifetime value as in the regular CLV calculation.

There are many ways one can try to be faithful to the retention decisions (and consumption values) in the held out data. The aim of the validation exercise is to be as close as possible in using these data in constructing the expected profits from our method. This is most likely to give the best comparison with the real observed profits for the customer.

The key takeaway from this validation model is that even a simple spreadsheet model can be developed and validated with a reasonable amount of data without any involved computer programming, to quickly give insights into the potential lift obtainable from existing data.

Key Skills to Master

- *Understand the basic principle of dynamic optimization.*
- *Experiment with different consumption model specifications, and understand how the resulting numbers in the model for the firm's action change and how the total profit is affected.*
- *Recognize that the solution from the dynamic optimization framework is a sequence of adaptive firm actions (or customer treatments) that are customized.*

Exercises

1. **Firm optimization via dynamic programming:** Suppose that the log-linear consumption for customer i in period t is given by the following trend:

$$\log C_{it} = 1.18 \cdot \log C_{it-1} - 0.2 \cdot T_{it} + 0.07 \cdot Y_{it} + 0.1 \cdot Z_{it} + 0.43$$

Here $\log C_{it}$ is the log-consumption of the same customer in the period number t (if period t is the first period, then $\log C_{it-1}$ is set to 0). The term $T(i,t)$ is tenure or simply t (as in exercise 1 in chapter 3) and the variables W, X, Y, and Z, are as in the original Facespace data set. A_{it} is set to 1 if the marketing action is performed on customer i in period t.

Customer i's utility in period t, denoted U_{it}, is the following linear function:

$$U_{it} = 3.55 \cdot A_{it} + 0.03 \cdot C_{it} + 0.55 \cdot W_{it} + 0.35 \cdot X_{it} + 1.25 \cdot Y_{it} - 5.15$$

Furthermore, the customer retention behavior is modeled by a random linear utility with extreme value noise, so the probability that customer i is retained in period t (so as to carry over to period $t+1$) is

$$\frac{e^{U_{it}}}{1 + e^{U_{it}}}$$

In this exercise, we restrict attention to a single customer i having the following values of the W, X, Y, Z variables (over time periods 1 through 10):

Time t	1	2	3	4	5	6	7	8	9	10
T_{it}	0	1	2	3	4	5	6	7	8	9
W_{it}	1	1	1	1	1	1	1	1	1	1
X_{it}	2	2	2	2	2	2	2	2	2	2
Y_{it}	2.72	2.10	2.63	2.31	2.66	2.01	2.75	2.52	2.40	2.55
Z_{it}	0.44	0.44	0.63	0.27	0.19	0.97	0.16	0.73	0.68	0.70

Assume that the log of the customer's current consumption is $\log_{10} C_{it} = 0.5$.

Facespace gets a fee of \$10 from customer i in every period as long as the customer retains service, and the cost of a marketing action (in any period) is \$3. Assume a discount factor of 0.97 from each period to the next. Extend the basic optimization shell to find the best sequence of actions to perform on customer i, so as to maximize the customer's lifetime value to Facespace. What is the resulting expected lifetime value for this customer if Facespace were to make optimal marketing decisions?

2. **Adding marginal costs to the firm's optimization:** Consider the same consumption and retention model as in the previous exercise, and also the same customer i (with the W, X, Y, Z, variables as given in the table above). Also assume, as before, that the log of the customer's current consumption $\log_{10} C_{it} = 0.5$.

The previous problem assumed that the only cost to Facespace was the marketing action (of $3 for each action). Now, enhance this model by taking into account a per-unit consumption cost of $0.2 that is incurred by Facespace. Continue to use $10 as the periodic fee that is paid by the customer, $3 as the action cost, and 0.97 as the discount rate. For example, if the customer consumes 15 units in period 1 and Facespace sends a marketing action, the profit to Facespace in this period is $4.

3. **Using CLV in campaigns:** Suggest some ideas for incorporating the CLV model we developed above for a customer-centric firm's optimization problem for the more traditional campaign-centric framework. For example, if we have a budget for sending promotions to a limited set of customers, how could you use the ideas in the framework we developed, to select which customers to send the promotions to?

4. **Firm optimization models for the cases:** For each of the four cases, answer the following questions about the setup of the firm's optimization problem.

   a. What is the objective function for your final optimization model? How do all the estimated components feature in it? How do the different marketing actions you have at your control influence the objective function? Will you use maximization or minimization to find the best results for your business objectives, or would you be using optimization to achieve some target value for the objective? Explain this in detail.

   b. How can you test the validity of your optimization objective? What experiments can you run on any data you decide to hold out, to do a counterfactual study of the effectiveness of your model?

   c. Did you perform a latent class segmentation estimation for your project data set? Does it make sense to perform this not only for the choice variable but also for the consumption variable in your project? If you carried out either of these, what distinguishing features do you expect for different clusters?

   d. How do the latent class segments you found modify your optimization approach? How can you validate their inclusion in the optimization process?

Examples

Amazon Automates the Journey from First Click to Final Purchase

How does one segment web shoppers in order to target them better? As a group, they are amorphous, but as individuals, they are different from one another in their buying preferences. The basis of segmentation should be on the benefits the customers are seeking—perceived and real—rather than on conventional bases of segmentation like demographics.

Amazon.com has an encyclopedic knowledge of the company's enormous stock and a perfect recall of what customers purchased in the past, and the ability to make well-informed recommendations. It recognizes four expectations from customers with regard to their online experience—physical, cognitive, emotional, and synaptic—and has incorporated all the four features accordingly.

The website has a presentable appearance that is user-friendly. It has a built-in capability to delineate patterns, help draw quick conclusions, and communicate them effectively to shoppers on the go. It is attentive to the requests of a shopper and mindful of the shopper's time, which helps build a rapport. The tools are easy to navigate. They provide recommendations more clinically than an experienced and well-trained employee would normally provide. The website is also well connected to other relevant resources at Amazon.com.

When a visitor adds a product to her shopping cart but does not complete the purchase, the website sends an automated email inviting her to review the shopping cart and recommending, at the same time, complementary products. When a visitor views various products in a category but does not buy any of them, it sends her an email that features top sellers from the category, while also offering relevant purchase options.

Kimberly-Clark Evaluates Payback from Promotions

Its vast retailer promotion operations were often a pain point for Kimberly-Clark, one of the leading consumer packaged-goods companies. It was unable to gauge the success of promotions it was running in thousands every year. The company had only the aggregate numbers on trade promotions. It could not break them down by individual customer, product, or shipment.[2]

Kimberly-Clark addressed the problem by building onto an existing software program for account management, which its sales department had developed to track investments in individual promotion efforts. The enhanced system, called Business Planner, integrated the program with shipment data. It soon became central to the company's sales and marketing efforts around 2,300 promotional schemes of the company's consumer product lines. Salespeople in the field used it to design promotional packages on-site for specific retailers. Marketing staff used it to plot broader promotion plans. Business Planner armed customer account managers with consistent data that helped change their perspective— from managing an account to managing the business.

Building on the success of Business Planner software, Kimberly-Clark is now implementing a more ambitious system designed to reach beyond its retailer customers into a wide array of consumer advertising and promotional activities. The enhanced suite, called Brand Builder, helps the company plan and evaluate the success of individual activities—a freestanding coupon inserted into the Sunday papers, for instance—and measure the combined effect of a number of integrated activities. The Brand Builder suite consists of a state-of-the-art collaborative tool that lets sales agents, designers, vendors, and retailers plan promotions online. It brings up, in real time, information learned about consumers online. And by integrating promotional-spending data with scanner and financial information, it provides a powerful analytical tool.

Kimberly-Clark has moved from relieving a pain point for its retailer customers to making a science of marketing. The company now knows, for example, that the payback for some consumer promotion programs is twice as high as for others intended to produce the same results. With that kind of information, the firm can identify which elements of marketing—coupon value or creative impact, for instance—result in higher returns.

7 Continuous Learning and Adaptive Marketing Decisions

Key Ideas

- The dynamic optimization framework can be expanded to allow learning by doing. A firm can accrue customer information regularly and improve its knowledge of customers continuously.

- Incorporating adaptive learning into the dynamic optimization framework allows the firm to update its belief based on the feedback collected from the most recent firm-customer interaction. It also allows the firm to "experiment" with improving the accuracy of its knowledge of customers.

- Adaptive learning and adaptive marketing decisions enable the firm to improve its relationship with the customers in a timely fashion.

- Currently, adaptive learning is more an idea than a technique. With increasing adoption of software-based decision support systems, we will see the gradual realization of this promising idea.

In this chapter, we extend our optimization method to incorporate continuous improvement of the firm's knowledge on customer preference and constant revision of firm's actions; we term these adaptive learning and adaptive marketing decision making respectively.

Accruing Customer Information in Real Time

The segmentation approach, which has been in vogue for years now, uses historical data to classify customers. It is based primarily on a snapshot of demographic variables. It treats customers as static.

However, technology makes it possible today for a firm to collect information of individual customers from various digital platforms in a dynamic way. Structured and unstructured data, containing valuable information on each individual customer, are accruing every moment. Furthermore, due to the proliferation of multiple digital touchpoints, consumers are continuously interacting with firms and brands not only by purchasing, but also by commenting in social media and engaging in two-way communications with the firms and brands.

Many firms have therefore set up an online presence around brand communities to continuously engage with their customers. The feedback from customers about their most recent interactions with firms reveals valuable and unique information about each individual customer. However, companies are far from leveraging such customer information fully.

Learning Continuously

A firm's knowledge of an individual customer is never complete and accurate. It is a matter of constantly reducing uncertainty and improving accuracy. Furthermore, customer preferences and needs evolve over time. It is important for the firm to follow their choices and continuously update its knowledge so as to make more accurate marketing actions. Below are a few examples of some common types of customer preferences and needs that must be updated continuously.

First, customer sensitivities to a firm's marketing variables change over time. This is particularly true of long-term relationships where customers change their sensitivities to predictive variables such as product offerings, prices, promotions, and channels. It is important to learn these changes in sensitivities in order to offer more customized products, targeted deals and discounts.

Second, customers may have different levels of preference for different communication channels.[1] Since the 1990s, firms have been racing to add twenty-four-hour call centers, direct mail, email, fax, Web page forms, and social media to their service channels. They are also focusing on service channels that encourage automated self-service such as Internet information services, voice-recognition phone systems, and transaction kiosks. Each customer may have a different preference in different steps of her decision process, such as information search, purchase, transaction, and post-purchase service.[2] Managers face some dilemmas here. How do we successfully blend the functions of multiple communication channels? How do we steer customers to their most preferred channels? How do we direct self-sufficient customers toward self-learning channels? Given the high cost of customer communication, it is important to identify the channel prefer- ences of customers. This will ensure optimal allocation of resources and also improve the effectiveness and efficiency of CRM interventions.

Third, marketing interventions help increase purchase frequency and trigger immediate sales for the firm. They also help educate customers to anticipate their own needs. It is therefore important to understand a customer's status before sending him promotional campaigns. For example, Li, Sun, and Montgomery (2005) have developed a stochastic dynamic optimization framework with hid- den Markov models to capture the evolution of customer financial maturity. They provide empirical evidence to suggest that CRM campaigns educate custom- ers about what products can satisfy their financial needs well before the custom- ers themselves are aware of their needs. For example, a firm could use data mining to characterize the behavior surrounding a life-changing event like retire- ment, and send informative campaigns to those nearing retirement to prepare them better for the event.

Fourth, a key purpose of developing customer relationships is for the company to cross-sell additional products and services to existing customers. To achieve this, companies need to learn about the development of individual customer demand.[3] The customer demand for various products is governed by a latent and evolving demand state (or maturity). The latter develops over time, due to factors like changes in life-stages, accumulation of consumption experience, availability of financial resources, and awareness of particular products. The evolving—but latent—demand maturity represents an individual customer's readiness for a particular product at a certain time. It is an important predictor for products that are most likely to be purchased at a certain time by a particular customer. An accurate knowledge of the development of each individual customer's demand is crucial for improving the targeting effectiveness of cross-selling campaigns.

Fifth, it is important to predict CLV because it relates directly to customer revenue, cost of acquisition, and customer profitability. CLV refers to the poten- tial revenue obtained from a customer during her relationship with a firm. Firms invest in customer relationships in order to increase long-term customer revenue in (at least) three ways: (1) increase the purchases of products customers already have; (2) sell them more or higher-margin products; and (3) retain the customers for a longer period of time. In addition, managers need to track and compute the cost of acquiring each customer and relate the cost to the profits the customer could generate for the firm over his lifetime. Knowing future profitability serves two functions: it helps calculate future discounted value of existing customers without intervention (as documented by CLV analysis in most existing marketing literature), and it estimates the impact of current marketing intervention on future customer value (as we advocate here).

Adaptive Learning and Adaptive Marketing Action are Two Iterative Steps of The Dynamic Optimization Process

When the idea of adaptive learning is integrated into the dynamic optimization framework, it enables adaptive marketing decision making as the firm's decision in each period of time is made based on the most updated knowledge about each individual customer using real-time customer information. Each marketing action is adaptive to the evolution of the path of each individual customer.

Adaptive learning and adaptive marketing decision making are two iterative steps that are integrated into the dynamic programming approach. Their incorporation has the following characteristics: (1) the accrued real-time information is used to continuously update the company's knowledge of the customer's preferences; (2) the company's strategic decision is adapted according to the updated knowledge; (3) as a result, the company can revise its belief in the next period based on the successful (or unsuccessful) interactions with the customer.

We term this type of learning as "adaptive marketing."[4] It offers the company an opportunity to learn about customer preferences and adapt its strategies in real time. It is an important class of learning algorithms in an environment with randomness.

With the improvement in the accuracy of its knowledge of customer preferences, a firm can not only serve its customers better, but also retain them. It can also improve the effectiveness of its interactions with customers. Thus, by following the signature of a customer's development, adaptive learning is more aligned with the idea of customer-centric marketing with the goal of proactively managing relationships for long-term profit. Should the business environment change—due to competitive dynamics, customer sensitivity to price, or service quality—adaptive marketing ensures that such a change is factored into the firm's response.

The concept of adaptive learning is consistent with the concept of organizational learning that focuses on using prior successes as the basis for developing future strategies.[5] Firms use adaptive learning to make incremental improvements to existing products, services, and processes in response to the changing business environment.

The idea of adaptive marketing is consistent with and implements the concepts of prescriptive analytics. Prescriptive analytics not only anticipates what will happen and when it will happen, but also suggests decision options on how to take advantage of a future opportunity or mitigate a future risk. It shows the implication of each decision option. Prescriptive analytics can continually take in new data to re-predict and re-prescribe, thereby improving the accuracy of prediction and prescribing better decision options. Thus we can interpret adaptive learning as a prototypical use of the prescriptive analytics paradigm in marketing.

Adaptive marketing has a compelling value proposition: it is situation-agnostic. Its core elements have universal relevance. They can be applied across industries.

Comparing Passive Learning and Adaptive Learning

Customer segmentation models as described in chapter 4, typical of CRM initiatives, help econometricians build a snapshot of a customer's sensitivities to marketing variables. We term this type of learning as "passive learning" because the segmentation is based on pooled historical data, and inferences are made in an ad hoc fashion.

Consider Amazon.com as an example. The online bookseller has a recommendation system in place that is meant to increase sales by deploying cross-customer analysis. The underlying assumption is that customers with similar demographics and purchase history own similar products. Products to be cross-sold are thus recommended based on the snap shot of purchasing behavior of all other customers. The system at Amazon.com is based on a giant matrix characterizing the correlations among millions of products. The recommendation is based on cross-product comparison that is offered by big data analysis. They are aimed at predicting the next-to-be-purchased product (from the customer's point of view) in a cross-selling situation rather than the-best-product-to-be cross-sold (from the firm's point of view).[6] The interaction of recommendations with the development of the customer is not taken into account.

Our proposed adaptive marketing framework values detailed and real-time customer information. And, it advocates that decision-making should reflect the development path of each individual customer. To make Amazon's recommendation system adaptive, the recommendation system should utilize the customer's reaction to the last time a book was recommended. Thus, different books should be recommended to a customer who viewed the recommended book than to the one who did not. In other words, adaptive marketing decision should factor in real-time interactions with customers.

Adaptive learning can be integrated into the firm's dynamic optimization problem. Starting from the membership probabilities resulting from the latent class estimates, the dynamic optimization problem can be built to continuously update the firm's belief on each individual customer's segment membership using information collected from each recent interaction. This way, as time goes on, the improved accuracy of the firm's knowledge allows the firm to adapt its marketing decisions to the preference of each individual customer. Adaptive learning differs from passive learning in the following ways: First, adaptive learning refers to the case of a company being identified as a decision maker that is actively gaining knowledge about customers. In passive learning, it is the econometricians who set the agenda for learning about customer heterogeneity. Models with passive learning do not treat companies as CRM decision makers. Second, adaptive learning follows a development path in gaining customer knowledge. Passive learning relies on a snapshot of cross-customer comparisons. Third, adaptive learning occurs in real-time. Passive learning happens after the fact. Fourth, the knowledge gained from adaptive learning is dynamic, since it is updated with the last executed decision. The knowledge gained from passive learning is static, since it crucially ignores the customer reactions to the company's most recent interventions.[7]

An Example of Adaptive Learning of Customer Heterogeneous Preference

We use the call allocation case from chapter 2 as an example to illustrate the basic idea of adaptive learning and how it is integrated into the dynamic optimization framework.[8] More specifically, we use the estimation of latent classes as the prior probabilities for each customer belonging to each of the segments. We then incorporate the adaptive learning feature into the optimization framework. As we continue to engage with a particular customer and the continuous interactions are documented in a CRM data system, we can refine the probability that she is from a particular segment by using Bayesian learning. The update will allow us to more accurately "learn" the latent class she is from, with repeated interactions. We already saw an example of this kind of learning update about segment membership toward the end of chapter 4 on latent class segmentation.

Many Fortune 500 firms use offshore service centers to handle service calls from their customers. Some customers view offshore calls as a sign of disengagement on the part of the firm and are likely to leave the firm. Thus, it is imperative for the firm to identify such customers so that it can avoid routing calls from them to offshore centers for processing. To improve customer experience with the firm and use offshore service centers more effectively, the firm can better match each service call with the right center, according to individual customer preferences.

We therefore formulate the service allocation decisions of a firm as solutions to a stochastic dynamic programming problem, in which the firm iteratively learns about customer preferences and adapts its allocation decisions to the best of its knowledge so that it can maximize long-term, expected profits. In this framework, when evaluating the allocation decision A_{ijt} ($A_{ijt} = 1$ represents that when customer i calls in at time t, the firm will allocate her service center j with $j = 1$ denoting onshore centers and $j = 0$ denoting offshore centers), the firm must calculate the expected service costs on the basis of the expected service duration and marketing consequences entailing customer retention.

To take into account the fact that companies usually conduct segmentation analysis based on demographic variables and know the average probabilities of a customer belonging to a segment, we define the prior belief of customer type $\Pr_{i0}(m)$ as the probability of segment membership resulting from the latent class approach in the estimation. This snapshot segmentation of customers is based on cross-customer comparisons and offers average probabilities of segment membership. These prior beliefs will be treated as the starting values in the firm's dynamic optimization problem.

As the firm starts to interact with individual customer (as represented in the dynamic programing problem), it can accrue information by observing the customer feedback to the firm's most recent interventions. There are at least two sources from which information is accrued. The first is the observed prior service durations because the same customer usually shows a consistent pattern over time in terms of the length of service durations. For example, retired customers have more time to talk on the phone and incur longer service durations. The second source is observed customer retention, which reveals customer preference by reflecting customer reactions to service allocations, and the resulting service treatments. For example, if being serviced by an offshore center leads a customer to leave the firm, this implies that this customer is very sensitive to this treatment.

Similarly, when a long service duration leads a customer to leave the firm, it shows that this customer reacts negatively to wait times.

Assuming customers' preferences do not change over time, we let the firm learn about the possibility of a customer belonging to segment or type m, or $\Pr_{it}(m)$ for $m = 1, \ldots, M$. Let $LR_{it}(m = n)$ denote the ratio of the probability of customer i belonging to $m = n$ type, relative to that of $m = 1$ type, perceived by the firm at time t (LR stands for likelihood ratio). According to the Bayesian rule of learning, the firm's perceived likelihood ratio of the consumer belonging to type $m = n$ relative to $m = 1$ is given by the following update equation.

$$LR_{it}(m = n) = \frac{\Pr_{it}(m = n)}{\Pr_{it}(m = 1)} = LR_{it-1}(m = n) \frac{\Pr(DUR_{ijt-1} \mid m = n)}{\Pr(DUR_{ijt-1} \mid m = 1)} \frac{\Pr(RET_{it-1} \mid m = n)}{\Pr(RET_{it-1} \mid m = 1)}$$

for $m = 1, \ldots, M$. The intuition is as follows: At the beginning of time t, the firm observes new information realized between $t - 1$ and t, namely, the duration DUR_{ijt-1} and customer attrition RET_{it-1}. The firm calculates the probabilities of the observed service duration and that of the observed retention according to the estimated equations for all customer types $m = 1, \ldots, M$. When the joint probability of observing $DUR_{ij(t-1)}$ and RET_{it-1}, under the assumption that customer i belongs to segment $m = n$, is greater than that under the assumption that he or she belongs to segment $m = 1$ or

$$\frac{\Pr(DUR_{ijt-1} \mid m = n) \cdot \Pr(RET_{ijt-1} \mid m = n)}{\Pr(DUR_{ijt-1} \mid m = 1) \cdot \Pr(RET_{ijt-1} \mid m = 1)} > 1$$

the likelihood that customer i belongs to $m = n$ group increases. In other words, when the observed duration and resulting retention are more likely when the customer is assigned to segment m, the firm increases its belief that this customer belongs to segment m. When customers do not call in,

$$\frac{\Pr(DUR_{ijt-1} \mid m = n)}{\Pr(DUR_{ijt-1} \mid m = 1)} = 1$$

the belief is updated solely on the basis of observed retention. Given the updating rule, for all $m = 1, \ldots, M$, the perceived probability that customer i belongs to type m at time t is given by

$$\Pr_{it}(m = n) = \frac{LR_{it}(m = n)}{\sum_{m=1}^{M} LR_{it}(m)}$$

In the above updating process, the feedback collected from each customer interaction is used to improve the accuracy of the belief that a customer belongs to the segment that is sensitive to offshore centers. The probability of segment membership given by the latent class approach only serves as an initial belief. From there, adaptive learning enables a continuous learning process and can be built into the dynamic optimization problem. The learning process allows the firm to use accrued information to continuously update its beliefs about the customer's intrinsic type. The updated knowledge is used to adjust allocation decisions, and the resulting customer reactions are fed back into the updating process in the proposed framework. Adaptive learning thus allows the firm to improve its relationship with the customers in a timely fashion.

This example demonstrates adaptive learning about customer types. Similar models can be developed to allow for other types of adaptive learning as listed at the beginning of this chapter.

Recall that we incorporated such an active learning update in the solved version LC-BLE.xls: it contained a final column illustrating a simple example of Bayesian update to determine which of the two segments each customer is from. We went through exactly the same process, detailed above, to revise the information about the customer's segment as we get more and more interaction data from her.

Incorporating Latent Customer Classes in Firm's Optimization

We now explain how our dynamic optimization framework can be extended to allow the firm to continuously revise its belief on the membership of segmentation, and adapt its marketing intervention decisions to its most updated information.

If we suspect that the customers fall into several latent classes and that they must be handled differently in setting up the firm's optimization problem, we can extend the optimization method to address this. As before, we first estimate the consumption and retention trend coefficients. We can start with a single estimation of the coefficients for the log-linear consumption model regardless of which segment the customer in the data may actually belong to. We thus assume that all customers have the same consumption pattern, independent of the segment they come from. This leads to a decoupling of the estimations of the consumption coefficients and of the retention probability.

The methods are detailed in the "LCOptShell.xlsx" workbook in the first LC-Est worksheet. Note that since we require panel data for segment estimation, but some customers are not retained through the whole set of ten periods, we do not have consumption data for every customer for every period. However, if we assume that the random linear utility used in the logistic retention function is a function of both the marketing action and the consumption (as denoted by Action and B respectively in this sheet), we will need a value for the as-yet-unknown consumption B at each period even for nonretained customers. We can estimate the growth of the consumption values in this step and compute interpolated B-values that we fill and use in predicting the probability of retention. This is carried out in the first workbook.

The second workbook in LCOptShell titled "opt" addresses the generalization of the optimization model. It is straightforward and duplicates the single segment optimization model into two copies, one for each segment: the top model for segment 1 uses the b-coefficients for the retention probability function from the first segment while the lower model uses the second segment coefficient values. Thus, the two models could lead to different decisions about the marketing action. To determine which of these to use, we simply compute the probability that the current customer is from each segment and use the result for the more likely one.[9] These computations are detailed in the second worksheet.

The filled-in version "LC-Opt.xlsx" contains the fully worked out values. You should consult this only after you have tried to work out the coefficients on your own from the first shell. Note that when using the model we have built with any new customer, we can actually use the known current consumption value for this period and extrapolate the future consumption values going forward. Any other customer-specific features of the model (such as the use of some demographic information in the consumption or retention relationships) can be initialized with the observed value for the current customer on whom we are trying to apply this model. It allows us to completely use what we know about customers in our current decision-making procedure.

Another important point to note is the adaptive revision of a belief of the customer's latent class. As in chapter 4 on segmentation, while we continue to observe more and more data (on say, consumption or retention) on the customer, we can revise our estimate of the probability that the customer is from a particular segment (say 1). Even if we start with two demographically similar customers with identical initial consumption and retention patterns, it is possible, as the relationship with them grows, to put them in two different "latent" segments based on their behavior. This adaptive response of the firm to the changing consumer behavior is a unique element of the approach we advocate.

Experimentation to Speed Up the Learning

As explained at the beginning of the book, experimentation is one of the four salient features of the optimal solution when trading off exploration of customer preference and exploitation of profit contribution of each individual customer throughout a customer's lifetime. For example, without knowing anything about the new buyers, Amazon.com can randomly recommend a few books to a sample of buyers and measure their responses for the purpose of learning about their preference and evaluating the current recommendation system. Based on the reactions from the buyers in the following period, our proposed framework allows Amazon to immediately update its knowledge on these buyers and adjust its recommendation in the next period. At a small and immediate cost, the experimentation allows the company to improve its recommendation system in real time. Moreover, customer reaction to this new offer will be counted as input to the firm's learning process. This process continues until the gain of learning does not justify the cost of doing so.

When a firm has incomplete knowledge of a particular consumer, it is optimal for the firm to conduct experiments on demand in order to collect more information to enable more informed decisions in the future. Even though the experimentation may cause the firm a short-term loss, the firm will benefit in the long run, due to reduction in uncertainty or more knowledge of the consumer; this helps the firm make more informed decisions in the future and thus better serve the customer and make him or her stay and purchase more. Note that it is costly to run experiments. In our framework, when and on whom to run the experiment is optimally determined by taking into account the cost to the firm and potential benefit of knowing more about each individual consumer.[10]

The speed of learning is also endogenized in our optimization framework. Learning is part of the decision process that can facilitate data collection. For example, when the firm can learn faster by inducing the customer to buy more units of services, it should provide discounts to unfamiliar customers to explore the potential that they may be profitable customers. This offers an alternative explanation to the common observation that some firms, especially those with some monopoly power, such as the cable industry, offer promotional prices to new customers but keep the price high for their existing customers.

Recently, digital technology allows firms to easily run experimentation to test the effectiveness of their marketing decisions. For example, the popular A/B test assigns two different price levels to two very similar (randomly assigned) groups of consumers and determines the effectiveness of the price points based on sales. While this experimentation is valuable, it is usually done infrequently and in an ad hoc way. Our solution framework is consistent with the idea of A/B tests but allows a sophisticated version of "experimentation" that is automatically and proactively integrated into the firm's optimal decision. In addition, while A/B testing involves a time period when such tests are run, our framework incorporates this whenever the customer interacts with the firm (in "real time"). In these two ways, the extent to which experimentation is integrated into our framework is more sophisticated than A/B testing. Furthermore, A/B test is more suitable for evaluating a marketing strategy such as price for a mass market while our framework addresses comparing the effectiveness of two treatments for serving each individual customer.

Tools of Adaptive Learning and Adaptive Marketing Decisions

Continuous learning using real-time data is similar to Bayesian updating, wherein accruing customer information is used to update the company's knowledge of its customers. Thus, all the consumer learning models existing in the marketing literature can be modified in this context.

Data mining and machine learning can also serve as the basis for adaptive learning. These techniques combine algorithms developed in computer science with statistical techniques, to automatically search for patterns in large data sets. In the last decade, its commercial use has caught on in a big way due to the availability of large volumes of data, dramatic improvement of computing power, and growing competition. A number of software providers offer data-mining tools currently: RapidMiner, IBM SPSS and Cognos, and SAS.[11] However, data mining techniques are still of the passive learning kind unless they are modified to have the three characteristics specified in the definition of adaptive learning.

Proactive adaptive marketing decision making is a more sophisticated solution for developing relationships. Experience has shown that the best way to improve learning is to respond to clearly identified needs with clearly articulated solutions. Inferential tools like those we describe provide the giant step in using technology to improve learning to make it adaptive.

Skills to Master

- *Incorporate information about customer segment membership in the optimization problem.*

- *As more customer information accrues, revise the latent segment membership probabilities, thus adaptively learning the change in customer behavior and using that in the optimization of marketing actions.*

Examples

Tesco plc Decentralizes Data

Tesco plc is UK's largest grocery merchandiser, focused on fresh foods. It has what it calls a "signal advantage" among its global peers—an ability to capture, interpret, and act upon signals from rich, dynamic data in an unpredictable retail environment. Tesco hosts the United Kingdom's biggest loyalty program called the Clubcard with which it collects customer data. It uses the primary data, in turn, to make relevant offers in real time. The offers are designed to reward existing customers for their loyalty, rather than to wean away customers from competitors.

The company has recognized that an ability to collect data is less of an advantage than an ability to direct, filter, and work out what it would do with the data and fulfill on the customer value proposition. Tesco is moving away from its traditional information systems model of a central nervous system (which it sees as "dinosaur with the brain at the end of a very long neck") toward "distributive" nervous systems. The objective is to decentralize responsibilities and encourage more collaborative ways of working. Tesco is introducing flexibility in the way front end decisions are made (which are crucial to a retailer) within the rigor of protocols about "what information should go where."

AppLovin Leverages Advertiser Data to Deliver Personalized Experience

AppLovin is a nascent US company that uses data and predictive models to deliver dynamic advertisements on a mobile platform to individual customers. The adaptive personalization platform (APP), as it is called, allows brands to target users with marketing campaigns across multiple device types. The campaigns can be personalized at each of the 1.4 billion users of smartphones globally. The platform evolves as individual interests evolve, delivering campaigns suited to current tastes. The APP helps advertisers in not only making personalized recommendations to their customers but also in retargeting the reluctant ones and influencing their buying behavior. It enables them to keep their brands continually relevant to customers.

Advertisers have seen significant improvements in the metric they monitor closely—the mobile conversion rate. The use of the APP has enabled them to step up the rate from the traditional 3 percent to 10 percent.

8 Implications and Enablers

Key Ideas

- An integrated forward-looking optimization problem for the firm enables CCM.
- The result is a proactive, experimental, forward-looking and adaptive plan.
- Managers must recognize the value of long data and personalization, and take a long view in their CCM investments.

In this book, we formulate a firm's learning and decision-making processes as integrated solutions to a stochastic, dynamic programming problem. Our framework allows the firm, as a decision-maker, to learn about individual customer preferences, predict the consequences associated with each of the firm's interventions, calculate the long-term profit implications of each intervention, and choose a sequence of optimal interventions that maximize the sum of future profits.

Adaptive learning and proactive marketing, as formulated in our framework, enable firms to integrate data mining with analytical decision support systems. These learning and marketing tools help firms to continuously improve their knowledge of customers and adapt their decisions to maximize long-term profit. They empower firms to serve customers more effectively, reduce the cost of marketing and communication, and translate better customer knowledge into long-term profitability. With the emergence of software and web-based automated decision support systems, we anticipate that more and more firms will employ technologies that allow immediate access to customer databases, learn about customers' intrinsic preferences, and solve dynamic programming problems or their simplified versions to obtain optimal marketing intervention decisions.

The framework of our two-step procedure ("adaptive learning" and "proactive marketing decisions") implements the three components for customer-centric decision making (adaptive learning of an individual customer's preferences, forward-looking into future marketing consequences of current marketing interventions, and dynamic optimization to balance cost and benefit).

Real-time marketing decision-making and real-time delivery of CCM messages have become industry buzzwords. However, they are not about being in the moment and acting on what the firm knows about the customer in real time alone. They are about building long-term relations with the customer and using this knowledge in the context of marketing decision making, while balancing off cumulative marketing cost and customer revenue in the long run for the purpose of maximizing CLV.

The implementation of CCM requires the senior management to adjust their vision in the following ways.

Recognize the Value of Both Big and Long Data

The static segmentation approach that dominates current business practice has its limits. It renders the data that a firm has about individual customers obsolete and deficient. The data is subject to two kinds of errors: Type I error (wherein the firm provides services to the wrong customer) and Type II error (wherein the firm wrongly turns away profitable customers). They both lead to suboptimal decisions. Static segmentation involves trading off one type of error against the other. It also does not factor in the dynamic evolution of customers from one state to the other.

The ongoing data revolution has exponentially increased the amount of information available about each individual customer. It has also enabled highly interactive marketing communication environments. Firms should therefore recognize the importance of tracking the interactive history of each customer, especially when customers change their demand and preferences during the course of a long-term relationship with them. Learning from the feedback continuously collected from recent decisions enables firms to mitigate both Type I and Type II errors, improve the accuracy of customer identification, and track customer development. More important, firms should realize that acting on timely information is the ultimate means to realize the immediate and long-term value of information. This longitudinal data is especially valuable for cultivating customer relationship in the long run.

As Brian Wallace, the former VP of the Marketing at Samsung put it, "[Data] does not crush the art of advertising. It simply informs it—and ultimately improves it."

We have laid out in this book a plan to use existing data sources to achieve this improvement.

Be Ready to Forgo Short-Term Profit

A firm that acts myopically by caring only about current profits may not benefit from implementing learning. It must be forward looking on a longer horizon for its learning efforts to be fruitful. Learning might incur a short-term loss but the firm can benefit from more accurate customer information in the long run because of its improved ability to identify customer preferences and customization of its marketing decisions that it allows. As a result, customers are better served (effectiveness), and firms are better positioned to control their costs (efficiency), leading to higher long-term profits. Therefore, a firm implementing CCM should take a forward-looking view and be prepared to tolerate short-term financial losses during the early stages.

Not only does the result of learning improve a firm's marketing decisions, but the process of learning also affects a firm's day-to-day marketing strategies before the firm reaches a steady state. Learning enables a firm to take more risk and enter markets that, in spite of larger customer pools, may seem unprofitable. Firms should understand the pattern of intertemporal profit flow to estimate the amount and duration of short-term financial loss they will incur by learning. Accordingly, they can evaluate their investments and the payoff of implementing a CCM decision-making system.

Be the Butler of Each Individual Customer

Learning and acting on information gives the firm an ability to update its customer knowledge and improve its marketing strategies in a continuous fashion. Improved customer knowledge lets the firm act on information and tailor products or services to the preferences of each individual customer (or more practically, each segment). In addition, a forward-looking firm can take into account the future marketing consequences of its current marketing decisions.

Consequently, it will likely sacrifice its short-term profit, act proactively on customer information, and provide better service to maximize CLV. Its decision is customized and proactive, which is central to the idea of CCM. All these efforts enable a firm to create a smarter, more engaged customer experience at a lower cost, thereby improving customer loyalty, and hence, lifetime profit contribution to the firm.

CCM allows the firm to tailor its marketing offerings (product, advertising messages, price, promotion, channel, services etc.) to each customer's individual preference. It avoids treating customer as part of a "mass market" and driving the product to commodification, resulting in heightened competition and downward pressure on pricing.

Invest in Enabling Technology

In today's digital, Internet, and mobile world, a firm can deliver its marketing decisions to a specific customer just by knowing his first name, in real time, when he is engaged in "search and purchase" activities and at a location that is most relevant to its brand.

Taking coupon distribution as an example, a customer can receive the coupon offerings pushed to his mobile phone when he is getting closer to a particular product that he is most likely to purchase. The conceptual model we have described can be implemented as the back-end of such a system that monitors the changing effectiveness of such a coupon as the customer interaction with the firm evolves until the perfect moment when the offering will be most effective. By interfacing this system with modern updating engines, we can fully tap the promise of real-time marketing interactions with customers, the holy grail of marketing in this digital age.

Future Trends

Recent technological developments offer enormous possibilities for tracking the purchase history and collecting detailed information about each individual customer. However, customer information stored in a database will be of no value unless it is harnessed. The information cannot be transformed into profit unless the firm adapts its decisions to match its knowledge about individual customers. Realizing that customer information can create potential comparative advantages, as promised by CCM, firms have started to develop learning and interactive marketing strategies to explore the opportunities enabled by data collection, data mining, and decision-making technologies. Therefore, it calls for more advanced algorithms and systems to be developed to seamlessly integrate learning and marketing decision support tools.

Learning and acting on information helps a firm improve the accuracy of its knowledge about each customer and adapt its individualized marketing decisions on the basis of the most updated information. As a result, customers are better serviced and the service costs lowered, which then leads to improved profit. In addition, a firm with learning behaves more strategically than a firm without learning, because without learning, the firm will be better off serving only profitable customers from the beginning. In contrast, learning allows a firm to gradually identify and modify its marketing offering to unprofitable customers and match the right product to the right customer according to their preferences.

The approach we have proposed reveals what frontline marketers are doing to seamlessly integrate web and mobile technologies into their database marketing programs, and what you can do, starting now, to provide your best customers with recognition, service, friendship, and information—for which they will reward you with loyalty, and dramatically improve your sales and profits.

Skills to Master

- *Reflect on the real potential for utilizing long data to enable a CCM plan.*
- *Understand the hurdles and be prepared for the long haul in implementing a customer-centric marketing plan.*

Examples

Obama Campaigns Go for Adaptive Marketing
The election campaigns of Barrack Obama, during the US presidential polls of both 2008 and 2012, were characterized by the deployment of data-informed decision making and adaptive marketing. The digital strategy team recognized, early on, that getting very granular in their targeting was crucial to winning the election. By extracting voter files and collecting information via calls made to households every night, the team was able to identify the likelihood of electoral swings at the level of an individual household. It became the basis of determining the message relevant to each household and communicating it.

The Obama campaign expertly aimed targeted and personalized messaging via online advertising, email, door to door and phone canvassing. It also cleverly extended the strategy via social media. Nearly a million supporters who "liked" the Obama 2012 Facebook page also allowed access to their profile data via Facebook Connect. It enabled the campaign volunteers to identify their Facebook friends in battleground states, and cross-tabulate with their own databases. They then asked supporters to email or even personally call their friends who fit the typical Obama voter profiles, to remind them to register or vote early.

Virgin Atlantic Sees the Potential in Google Glass

In an industry in which customer expectations tend to be high, Virgin Atlantic is an innovator in managing expectations. It does so by deploying, among others, customer analytics. As the upper class VIP passengers disembark at Heathrow Airport and reach the arrival lounge, Virgin Atlantic agents identify them with the help of Google Glass devices they wear (like eye glasses) and greet them individually. They are checked in on a priority basis and provided with relevant information such as flight details, weather forecasts, and places to eat and visit. Since there is no need for agents to go behind a desk to look up something, they maintain eye contact with the passenger all the time, which Virgin Atlantic sees as crucial to the VIP customer experience.

Virgin Atlantic sees the potential in Google Glass for more accurate analytics of not only customer behavior, but also employee behavior and performance. The issues it is fine-tuning include the risk of sensitive customer data being intercepted in the event of an insecure connection, and the need for agents to stay natural without the customer getting a whiff of being "followed."

Google Glass is known to have a positive impact on employee productivity, which in turn improves customer service. Customers have attested to its effectiveness on grounds of feeling welcomed on arrival and going through a pleasant experience. Virgin Atlantic is planning to roll out Google Glass across all of its VIP concierge services.

Epilogue

We have focused in this book on describing an integrated framework by providing easy-to-use statistical tools, exercises, spreadsheets, cases, and illustrative examples.

We encourage readers who are interested in more analytical tools to read *The Marketing Information Revolution* by Robert Blattberg, Rashi Glazer and John Little (1994), *Principles of Marketing Engineering* by Gary L. Lilien, Arvind Rangaswamy and Arnaud De Bruyn (2012), and *Database Marketing: Analyzing and Managing Customers* by Robert C. Blattberg, Byung-Do Kim, and Scott A. Neslin (2008).

These books offer an excellent overview of key analytical, quantitative, and computer modeling techniques.

Notes

1   An Introduction to Customer-Centric Marketing

1. Blattberg and Deighton 1996; Haeckel 1998.

2. Peppers, Rogers, and Dorf 1999; Wind and Rangaswamy 2001; Rust, Lemon, and Zeithaml 2004.

3. Sheth et al. 2000.

4. Shugan 2004.

5. Winer 2001.

6. Cutler 2005.

7. Rossi, McCulloch, and Allenby 1996.

8. Berger et al. 2002.

9. Anderson and Salisbury 2003.

10. Kamakura, Ramaswami, and Srivastava 1991; Li, Sun, and Wilcox 2005.

11. Sun, Li, and Zhou 2006.

12. Kamakura and Russell 1989; Rossi, McCulloch, and Allenby 1996.

13. Shugan 2003.

14. Loveman 2003.

15. Lee and Whang 2006.

16. http://loblaw.ca/files/4.%20Investor%20Centre/Presentation%20Slides/2013/Loblaw%20-%20PC%20Plus%20Investor%20Teach-In_v001_p38t82.pdf (accessed September 13, 2015).

2   Conceptual Framework for Customer-Centric Marketing

1. Guadagni and Little 1983.

2. Venkatesan and Kumar 2004.

3. Edwards and Allenby 2003; Shankar, Smith, and Rangaswamy 2003; Li, Sun, and Wilcox 2005.

4. Interested readers can read Sun, Li, and Zhou 2006; Sun and Li 2011; and Li, Sun, and Montgomery, 2011 for more background information.

5. Sun, Li, and Sun 2015a.

6. The actual research used a hidden Markov model (HMM) that captures the customers' evolving needs and preferences (e.g., price and service quality) in their hidden relationship states with the company. We do not cover HMMs in this book but note that they are a natural extension of the consumer choice models and segmentation; we mention them here since they were effective in the study applying CCM to this problem.

7. The research used a HMM to capture the customers' evolving needs and preferences. The resulting dynamic optimization problem was a partially observable Markov decision process (POMDP) that accounts for customer heterogeneity.

8. The original research used hidden Markov transition states.

9. Cross-customer heterogeneity is captured by a hierarchical Bayesian framework in the actual implemented model.

10. Li, Sun, and Montgomery 2011.

11. Sun and Li 2011.

3   Modeling Consumer Choice

1. Train 2009.

2. Ibid.

3. Ibid.

4. All spreadsheets mentioned in the text are available online at mitpress.mit.edu/books/customer-centric-marketing.

5. We note that this estimation method is quite robust and gives converging values for the coefficients despite starting from different initial values for these coefficients, since the log-likelihood function is well behaved (concave) and has a single global maximum that is also the only locally maximum solution over the coefficients.

6. See Greene 2011 or Maddala and Lahiri 2009.

7. Train 2009.

8. Ibid.

9. Rayport and Jaworski 2004.

10. Parker and Chandrasekhar 2015.

4 Segmenting Customers into Latent Classes Based on Sensitivity

1. Kamakura and Russell 1989.

2. Berry and Linoff 2009.

3. Use the law of total probability:

$$P(A) = P(A \& B_1) + P(A \& B_2) + \ldots + P(A \& B_N), \ where \ B_1, B_2, \ldots, B_N$$

are mutually exclusive and collectively exhaustive.

4. Use the formula relating conditional and joint probabilities.

5 Customer Lifetime Value

1. Rajkumar and Kumar 2004.

2. Dixon, Freeman, and Toman 2010.

6 Marketing Optimization Problem

1. This section is somewhat more involved than the rest of the text and can be skipped without loss of continuity.

2. Rigby and Ledingham 2004.

7 Continuous Learning and Adaptive Marketing Decisions

1. Kumar, Venkatesan, and Reinartz 2008.

2. Ansari, Mela, and Neslin 2008; Sullivan and Thomas 2004.

3. Kamakura, Ramaswami, and Srivastava 1991; Li, Sun, and Wilcox 2005.

4. A similar idea has been adopted in conjoint analysis to reveal customer preferences as demonstrated by Toubia et al. (2003).

5. Sun and Li 2011.

6. Edwards and Allenby 2003.

7. Rust and Chung 2006.

8. Sun and Li 2011.

9. One might think of randomizing here by executing the action for the first segment with probability equal to the current estimate that this customer is from that segment and executing the marketing decision for the other segment with remaining probability, but this may lead to instability in the resulting outcomes and is not recommended.

10. A version of this is also called the "bandit problem" in the literature.

11. An updated list can be found at http://www.kdnuggets.com/software.

References

Allenby, Greg M., and Peter E. Rossi. 1999. "Marketing Models of Consumer Heterogeneity." *Journal of Econometrics* 89 (1/2): 57–78.

Anderson, Eugene, and Linda Court Salisbury. 2003. "The Formation of Market-Level Expectations and Its Covariates." *Journal of Consumer Research* 30 (1): 115–124.

Ansari, Asim, Carl F. Mela, and Scott A. Neslin. 2008. "Customer Channel Migration." *Journal of Marketing Research* 45 (1): 60–76.

Berger, Paul D., Ruth N. Bolton, Douglas Bowman, Elten Briggs, V. Kumar, A. Parasuraman, and Creed Terry. 2002. "Marketing Actions and the Value of Customer Assets: A Framework for Customer Asset Management." *Journal of Service Research* 5: 39–54.

Berger, Paul D., and Nada I. Nasr. 1998. "Customer Lifetime Value: Marketing Models and Applications." *Journal of Interactive Marketing* 12 (1): 17–30.

Berry, Michael, and Gordon Linoff. 2009. *Data Mining Techniques: Techniques: For Marketing, Sales, and Customer Support.* 3rd ed. Indianapolis, IN: John Wiley and Sons, Inc.

Blattberg, R., and J. Deighton. 1996. "Manage Marketing by the Customer Equity Test." *Harvard Business Review* 74 (4): 136–144.

Blattberg, R., Rashi Glazer, and John D. C. Little. 1994. *The Marketing Information Revolution.* Cambridge, MA: Harvard Business School Press.

Blattberg, R., B. D. Kim, and S. A. Neslin. 2008. *Database Marketing: Analyzing and Managing Customers.* New York: Springer.

Cao, Henry, and Baohong Sun. 2007. "Value of Learning and Acting upon Customer Information." Working Paper, Tepper School of Business. http://repository.cmu.edu/tepper/484/.

Cutler, Andy. 2005. "The Need for Customer-Centric Marketing." iMedia Connection (blog), August. http://www.imediaconnection.com/content/6537.asp (accessed June 2015).

Dixon, Matthew, Karen Freeman, and Nicholas Toman. 2010. "Stop Trying to Delight Your Customers." *Harvard Business Review* 88 (7/8): 4–8.

Du, Rex, and Wagner Kamakura. 2006. "Household Life Cycles and Lifestyles in the United States." *Journal of Marketing Research* 43 (1): 121–132.

Edwards, Y. D., and G. Allenby. 2003."Multivariate Analysis of Multiple Response Data." *Journal of Marketing Research* 40 (3): 321–334 .

Erdem, Tülin, and Michael P. Keane. 1996."Decision-Making under Uncertainty: Capturing Dynamic Brand Choice Processes in Turbulent Consumer Goods Markets." *Marketing Science* 15 (1): 1–20.

Greene, W. E. 2011. *Econonometric Analysis*. 7th ed. Upper Saddle River, NJ: Prentice Hall.

Guadagni, P., and J. Little. 1983. "A Logit Model of Brand Choice Calibrated on Scanner Data." *Marketing Science* 2 (3): 203–238.

Haeckel, Stephan H. 1998. "About the Nature and Future of Interactive Marketing." *Journal of Interactive Marketing* 12 (1): 63–71.

Kalyanaram, Gurumurthy, and Russell S. Winer. 1995. "Empirical Generalizations from Reference Price Research." *Marketing Science* 14 (3): 161–169.

Kamakura, Wagner, and Gary J. Russell. 1989. "A Probabilistic Choice Model for Market Segmentation." *Journal of Marketing Research* 26 (November): 379–390.

Kamakura, W., S. Ramaswami, and R. Srivastava. 1991. "Applying Latent Trait Analysis in the Evaluation of Prospects for Cross-Selling of Financial Services." *International Journal of Research in Marketing* 8: 329–349.

Keane, Michael P., and Kenneth I. Wolpin. 1994. "The Solution and Estimation of Discrete Choice Dynamic Programming Models by Simulation: Monte Carlo Evidence." *Review of Economics and Statistics* 76 (4): 648–672.

Kumar, V., Rajkumar Venkatesan, and Werner Reinartz. 2008. "Performance Implications of Adopting a Customer-Focused Sales Campaign." *Journal of Marketing* 72 (September): 50–68.

Lee, Hau, and Seungjin Whang. 2006. "Harrah's Entertainment Inc.: Real-Time CRM in a Service Supply Chain." Stanford Graduate School of Business Case GS-50, Palo Alto, CA.

Li, Shibo, John C. Liechty, and Alan L. Montgomery. 2005. "Modeling Category Viewership of Web Users with Multivariate Count Models." Indiana University Working Paper.

Li, Shibo, Baohong Sun, and Alan Montgomery. 2011. "Cross-Selling the Right Product to the Right Customer at the Right Time." *Journal of Marketing Research* 48 (4): 683–700.

Li, Shibo, Baohong Sun, and Ronald T. Wilcox. 2005. "Cross-Selling Sequentially Ordered Products: An Application to Consumer Banking Services." *Journal of Marketing Research* 42 (2): 233–239.

Lilien, Gary L., Arvind Rangaswamy, and Arnaud De Bruyn. 2012. *Principles of Marketing Engineering*. 2nd ed. State College, PA: DecisionPro, Inc.

Loveman, Gary. 2003. "Diamonds in the Data Mine." *Harvard Business Review* 81 (5): 109–113.

Maddala, G. S., and K. Lahiri. 2009. *Introduction to Econometrics*. 4th ed. Chichester, West Sussex, England: Wiley.

Montgomery, Alan L., Shibo Li, Kannan Srinivasan, and John C. Liechty. 2004. "Modeling Online Browsing and Path Analysis Using Clickstream Data." *Marketing Science* 23 (4): 579–595.

Moon, Sangkil, Wagner A. Kamakura, and Johannes Ledolter. 2007. "Estimating Promotion Response When Competitive Promotions Are Unobservable." *Journal of Marketing Research* 44 (3): 503–515.

Netzer, Oded, James M. Lattin, and V. Srinivasan. 2008. "A Hidden Markov Model of Customer Relationship Dynamics." *Marketing Science* 27 (2): 185–204.

Parker, Simon and Ramasastry Chandrasekhar. 2015. "Luminar: Leveraging Big Data using Corporate Entrepreneurship." https://www.iveycases.com/ProductView.aspx?id=66165.

Peppers, Don, Martha Rogers, and Bob Dorf. 1999. "Is Your Company Ready for One-to-One Marketing?" *Harvard Business Review* 77 (1): 151–160.

Venkatesan, Rajkumar, and V. Kumar. 2004. "A Customer Lifetime Value Framework for Customer Selection and Resource Allocation Strategy." *Journal of Marketing* 68 (October): 105–125.

Rayport, Jeffrey F., and Bernard J. Jaworski. 2004. "Best Face Forward." *Harvard Business Review* 82 (12): 47–52.

Reinartz, Werner, and V. Kumar. 2000. "On the Profitability of Long-Life Customers in a Noncontractural Setting: An Empirical Investigation and Implications for Marketing." *Journal of Marketing* 64 (4): 17–35.

Reinartz, Werner, and V. Kumar. 2003. "The Impact of Customer Relationship Characteristics on Profitable Lifetime Duration." *Journal of Marketing* 67 (January): 77–99.

Rigby, Darrell K., and Dianne Ledingham. 2004. "CRM Done Right." *Harvard Business Review* 82 (11): 118–129.

Rossi, Peter E., Robert E. McCulloch, and Greg M. Allenby. 1996. "The Value of Purchase History Data in Target Marketing." *Marketing Science* 15 (4): 321–340.

Rust, Roland T., Katherine N. Lemon, and Valarie A. Zeithaml. 2004. "Return on Marketing: Using Customer Equity to Focus Marketing Strategy." *Journal of Marketing* 68 (January): 109–127.

Rust, Roland T., and Tuck Siong Chung. 2006. "Marketing Models of Service and Relationships." *Marketing Science* 25 (6): 560–580.

Sawhney, Mohanbir, Sridhar Balasubramanian, and Vish Krishnan. 2004. "Creating Growth with Services, MIT." *MIT Sloan Management Review* 45 (2).

Shankar, Venkatesh, Amy Smith, and Arvind Rangaswamy. 2003. "The Relationship Between Customer Satisfaction and Loyalty in Online and Offline Environments." *International Journal of Research in Marketing* 20 (2): 153–175.

Sheth, N. Jagdish, Rajendra S. Sisodia, and Arun Sharma. 2000 "The Antecedents and Consequences of Customer-Centric Marketing." *Journal of the Academy of Marketing Science* 28: 55.

Shugan, Steven M. 2003. "Editorial: Defining Interesting Research Problems." *Marketing Science* 22 (1): 1–15.

Shugan, Steven. 2004. "The Impact of Advancing Technology on Marketing and Academic Research." *Marketing Science* 23 (4): 469–475.

Shugan, S. M., and J. H. Xie. 2000. "Advance Pricing of Services and Other Implications of Separating Purchase and Consumption." *Journal of Service Research* 2 (3): 227–239.

Sullivan, Ursula Y., and Jacquelyn S. Thomas. 2004. "Customer Migration: An Empirical Investigation across Multiple Channels." University of Illinois at Urbana–Champaign Working Paper 04-0112.

Sun, Baohong, and Shibo Li. 2011. "Learning and Acting upon Customer Information: A Simulation-Based Demonstration on Service Allocations with Offshore Centers." *Journal of Marketing Research* 48 (1): 72–86.

Sun, Yacheng, Shibo Li, and Baohong Sun. 2015a. "An Empirical Analysis of Consumer Purchase Decisions under Price-Discrimination Bucket Pricing." *Marketing Science* 34 (5): 646–668.

Sun, Yacheng, Shibo Li, and Baohong Sun. 2015b. "When Is the Juice Worth the Squeeze? An Empirical Study of Optimal Structuring of Win-Back Strategy in the Presence of Consumer Dynamics." University of Colorado Working Paper. http://gradworks.umi.com/33/19/3319929.html.

Sun, Baohong, Shibo Li, and Catherine Zhou. 2006. "'Adaptive' Learning and 'Proactive' Customer Relationship Management." *Journal of Interactive Marketing* 20 (3/4): 82–96.

Toubia, Olivier, Duncan I. Simester, John R. Hauser, and Ely Dahan. 2003. "Fast Polyhedral Adaptive Conjoint Estimation." *Marketing Science* 22 (3): 273–303.

Train, K. E. 2009. *Discrete Choice Models with Simulation*. 2nd ed. New York: Cambridge University Press.

Venkatesan, Rajikumar, and V. Kumar. 2004. "A Customer Lifetime Value Framework for Customer Selection and Resource Allocation Strategy." *Journal of Marketing* 68 (October): 106–125.

Winer, Russell. 2001. "A Framework for Customer Relationship Management." *California Management Review* 43 (4): 89–105.

Wind, Jerry, and Arvind Rangaswamy. 2001. "Customerization: The Next Revolution in Mass Customization." *Journal of Interactive Marketing* 15 (1): 13–32.

Index

AARP, 63–64
Adaptive learning, 109–110
  basics of customer-centric marketing
    and, 9, 15, 17–21, 29–32
  customer lifetime value (CLV) and, 66
  decision making and, 95–108
  heterogeneity and, 100–103
  optimization and, 85, 98–99
  passive learning and, 99–100, 106
  proactive approach and, 17
  recommendation systems and, 92, 99,
    105, 108
  speeding up, 105–106
  tools for, 106
Adaptive marketing decisions, 20
  advertising and, 107–108
  AppLovin and, 107–108
  brands and, 96, 107–108
  campaigns and, 97, 107
  competition and, 98, 106–107
  consumption and, 97, 103–104
  continuous learning and, 95–108
  customer lifetime value (CLV) and, 97–98
  customer loyalty and, 107
  customer preferences and, 95–102, 105
  decision making and, 21, 95–108, 110
  email and, 96
  information and, 95–107
  interactions and, 95–103
  latent classes and, 103–104
  optimization and, 95–103

  panel data and, 103
  price and, 96, 98, 105–106
  proactive approach and, 98, 106
  profit and, 97–98, 101, 105
  promotions and, 96
  real-time customer information accrual
    and, 95–96
  segmentation and, 95, 99–104, 107
  technology and, 96, 105–106
  Tesco and, 107
  tools for, 106
Adaptive personalization platform (APP),
  107–108
Advertising
  adaptive marketing decisions and,
    107–108
  consumer choice and, 49
  continuous learning and, 107–108
  educating customers and, 6, 28, 61, 97
  email and, 3, 6, 28–29, 52, 63–64, 74–75,
    92, 96, 113–114
  Entravision and, 49
  latent classes and, 64
  online, 113
  optimization and, 93
  reducing cost of, 13
  social media and, 6, 49, 74, 96, 114
  tailored, 7, 112
  too much, 3
Amazon, 92, 99–100, 105
AppLovin, 107–108

Bandit problem, 120n10
Bayesian models, 58, 100, 102–103, 106,
    118n9
Bell Canada, 75
Big data, vii, 7, 21, 43, 99, 110–111
Binary logit choice model, 34–36, 40–41,
    46, 53, 57
Blattberg, Robert, 115
Brands
    adaptive marketing decisions and, 96,
        107–108
    consumer choice and, 18, 40, 43, 61, 93,
        96, 107–108, 112
    continuous learning and, 96, 107–108
    latent classes and, 61
    optimization and, 93
    sensitivities and, 61
Bucket pricing, 22–24, 25t, 32

Call centers, 10, 29–30, 96
Call routing, 31–32, 75, 101
Campaigns
    adaptive marketing decisions and, 97,
        107
    basics of customer-centric marketing
        and, 4, 6–7, 9, 11, 22, 26–29
    continuous learning and, 97, 107
    cross-selling, 6, 22, 26–29, 32, 64, 97,
        99
    customer lifetime value (CLV) and, 91
    decision making and, 4
    email, 64
    latent classes and, 64
    optimization and, 87, 91
    political, 113–114
    promotions and, 29 (see also Promotions)
Carnegie Mellon University, ix
Casino industry, 9–11
Cheung Kong Graduate School of
    Business, ix
Clusters, 5, 49, 52, 60, 63, 91
Cognos, 106
Competition

adaptive marketing decisions and, 98,
    106–107
advantages in, 2, 12
casino industry and, 9–10
consumer choice and, 40
continuous learning and, 98, 106–107
coupons and, 12
price pressures and, 112
understanding customer needs and, 2
win-back strategies and, 24
Consumer choice
    advertising and, 49
    brands and, 18, 40, 43, 61, 93, 96,
        107–108, 112
    competition and, 40
    consumption and, 34–35, 37, 42–44, 47,
        49
    continuous learning and, 43
    coupons and, 44
    customer lifetime value (CLV) and, 34,
        40
    customer loyalty and, 43, 48
    customer preferences and, 42–43, 48
    Entravision and, 49
    estimation from scratch for, 40
    First Direct and, 48
    goodness of fit and, 39
    information and, 33, 36, 43, 47–49
    interactions and, 41
    logit models and, 33–36, 40–42, 44–47
    maximum likelihood estimation (MLE)
        and, 34, 36, 38, 44–46, 118n5
    multiple dependent variables and, 42
    panel data and, 33, 36–38
    price and, 34, 42–45
    promotions and, 41, 49
    quality and, 18, 21, 24, 26, 31, 43, 98,
        118
    regression analysis and, 33–34, 39,
        45–46
    single dependent variables and, 42
    technology and, 49
    utility and, 33–35, 39, 41–44, 46–47

Consumption
  adaptive marketing decisions and, 97, 103–104
  basics of customer-centric marketing and, 4, 21–24
  consumer choice and, 34–35, 37, 42–44, 47, 49
  continuous learning and, 97, 103–104
  customer lifetime value (CLV) and, 69–74
  latent classes and, 51–52, 60–61
  optimization and, 77–79, 82–91
Continuous learning
  acting upon customer information and, 5–6
  adaptive marketing decisions and, 95–108
  advertising and, 107–108
  basics of customer-centric marketing and, 1, 4–9, 15–23, 29–32
  brands and, 96, 107–108
  campaigns and, 97, 107
  competition and, 98, 106–107
  consumer choice and, 43
  consumption and, 97, 103–104
  customer lifetime value (CLV) and, 1, 66, 97–98
  customer loyalty and, 107
  customer preferences and, 95–102, 105
  decision making and, 95–108
  email and, 96
  information and, 95–107
  interactions and, 95–103
  latent classes and, 58, 103–104
  optimization and, 95–103
  panel data and, 103
  price and, 96, 98, 105–106
  proactive approach and, 98, 106
  profit and, 97–98, 101, 105
  promotions and, 96
  real-time customer information accrual and, 95–96

  segmentation and, 40, 49, 95, 99–104, 107
  self-service and, 96
  technology and, 96, 105–106
Control variables, 19, 42
Coupons
  competition and, 12
  consumer choice and, 44
  customer lifetime value (CLV) and, 73–75
  optimization and, 93
  promotions and, 12–14, 20, 44, 73–75, 93, 112
  smart phones and, 12–14
Cross-selling, 6, 22, 26–29, 32, 64, 97, 99
Curse of dimensionality, 19
Customer behavior, 10, 14, 18, 24, 107, 114
Customer-centric marketing (CCM), vii–viii
  benefits of, 1
  casino industry and, 9–11
  concept of, 2–3, 15–32
  continuous learning and, 5 (*see also* Continuous learning)
  coupons and, 12–14, 20, 44, 73–75, 93, 112
  customer loyalty and, 3, 6, 10, 12
  customer preferences and, 1, 4, 6–8, 24, 26–32
  databases and, 8–11, 49, 64, 109, 112–115
  future trends and, 112–113
  as information driven, 6–7 (*see also* Information)
  leveraging computing advantage for, 8–14
  marketing framework for, 15–32
  proactive advancement and, 19–21
  reasons for choosing, 3
  technology and, 2, 7–11
Customer education, 6, 28, 61, 97

Customer lifetime value (CLV), viii
  adaptive learning and, 15, 66, 97–98
  basics of customer-centric marketing
    and, 1, 11, 15–23, 26–27, 30–32
  Bell Canada and, 75
  bucket pricing and, 23
  calculation of, 65, 68t, 70, 72–74
  campaigns and, 91
  casino industry and, 11
  consumer choice and, 34, 40
  consumption and, 69–74
  continuous learning and, 1, 66, 97–98
  coupons and, 73–75
  cross-selling and, 27
  customer response and, 65
  decision making and, 77–89
  email and, 74–75
  forward-looking orientation and, 15–16,
    20–21, 65, 72, 77, 80
  information and, 65, 69
  interactions and, 72, 75
  latent classes and, 64
  maximization of, 1, 68, 112
  net present value (NPV) and, 20, 65
  optimization and, 72, 77–91, 110
  proactive approach and, 72, 75
  profit and, 66–75, 97–98
  promotions and, 74–75
  regression analysis and, 72–74
  Relay Foods and, 74–75
  revenue and, 68–72
  service call allocation and, 30
  static, 66–68
  tier structures and, 11
  Wachovia and, 64
  win-back strategies and, 26
Customer loyalty
  adaptive marketing decisions and, 107
  basics of customer-centric marketing
    and, 3, 6, 10, 12
  consumer choice and, 43, 48
  continuous learning and, 107
  latent classes and, 61

  loyalty programs and, 43, 107
  returning customers and, 48
  sensitivities and, 61
  smarter experience for, 112–113
  win-back strategies and, 24–26, 32
Customer preferences
  adaptive marketing decisions and,
    95–102, 105
  basics of customer-centric marketing
    and, 1, 4, 6–8, 24, 26–32
  consumer choice and, 42–43, 48
  continuous learning and, 95–102, 105
  enabling technology and, 112–113
  history tracking and, 110–111
  individual, 32, 112
  intrinsic, 42, 59, 61, 109
  latent classes and, 59, 61
  lifetime value and, 69
  optimization and, 92
  recommendation systems and, 92, 99,
    105, 108
  sensitivities and, 59, 61
Customer relationship management
  (CRM), 8–9, 17f, 57, 65, 97–100
Customer response
  basics of customer-centric marketing
    and, 18–24, 27–28, 30, 32
  bucket pricing and, 22–23
  cross-selling and, 27
  customer lifetime value (CLV) and, 65
  heterogeneity and, 19
  optimization and, 85
  service call allocation and, 30
  win-back strategies and, 24

Database Marketing: Analyzing and
  Managing Customers (Blattberg, Kim,
  and Neslin), 115
Databases, 8–11, 49, 64, 109, 112–115
Data revolution, 110–111
Decision making, 111
  adaptive marketing decisions and, 21,
    95–108, 110

campaign-centric, 4
consistency and, 18–19
consumer choice and, 49 (*see also*
  Consumer choice)
continuous learning and, 95–108
customer lifetime value (CLV) and,
  77–89
customized, 1, 4, 6, 8–9, 13, 19, 43,
  82–87, 89, 96, 112
data analysis and, 7–8
dynamic, 6, 23, 61, 82–87
experimental, 1, 6, 9, 109
First Direct and, 48
forward-looking orientation and, 20–21
latent classes and, 61
optimization and, 7, 77
proactive, 1, 4, 6, 9, 15–17, 20, 22, 26,
  29, 31, 52, 72, 75, 98, 106, 109–110,
  112
sensitivities and, 61
support systems and, 7–9, 95, 109
technology and, 8–9, 113
three components in, 4–5
tools for, 106
Decision trees, 52, 79–81
De Gruyn, Arnaud, 115
Discounts
  price, 34, 43–44, 63, 74–75, 96, 105
  time, 16, 18, 65–68, 79
Door-to-door campaigns, 113
Du, Rex, 61

Efficiency
  basics of customer-centric marketing
    and, 3, 8, 14, 27, 29–30
  cost control and, 111
  CRM interventions and, 97
  marketing initiatives and, 3
Email, 113–114
  adaptive marketing decisions and, 96
  continuous learning and, 96
  cross-selling and, 29b
  customer lifetime value (CLV) and, 74–75

customer preferences and, 28
  educating customers through, 28
  inactivity and, 63–64
  latent classes and, 52, 63–64
  optimization and, 92
  segmentation and, 52, 63–64
  unsolicited, 3
Entravision, 49

Facebook, 114
Facespace, 44, 73, 90–91
Feedback, 11, 18, 95–96, 101–102, 110
First contact resolution (FCR) scores,
  75
First Direct, 48
Fortune 500 firms, 101
Forward-looking orientation, 1, 32
  customer lifetime value (CLV) and,
    15–16, 20–21, 65, 72, 77, 80
  decision making and, 20–21
  optimization and, 4–5, 8–9, 77, 80,
    109–111
  predictions from, 4–5
  segmentation and, 111
Future trends, 112–113

Gaussian distribution, 78
Glazer, Rashi, 115
Goodness of fit, 39
Google Glass, 114

Harrah's, 9–11
Heterogeneity, 4–8, 18
  adaptive learning and, 100–103
  Bayesian model and, 118n8
  bucket pricing and, 23
  cross-selling and, 27–28
  customer response and, 19
  hidden Markov model (HMM) and,
    118n7
  service call allocation and, 30
  unobserved consumer, 51
  win-back strategies and, 24

Hidden Markov model (HMM), 61, 97,
    118nn6–8

IBM SPSS, 106
Income brackets, 20
Information
    acting upon customer data and, 5
    adaptive marketing decisions and,
        95–107
    basics of customer-centric marketing
        and, 1, 5–8, 10, 16–21, 24, 32
    Bayesian models and, 58, 100, 102–103,
        106, 118n9
    centralizing, 10–11
    computing power and, 1, 106
    consumer choice and, 33, 36, 43, 47–49
    continuous learning and, 95–107
    customer lifetime value (CLV) and, 65,
        69
    data analysis and, 1–2, 7–9, 11, 40, 47,
        99
    data mining and, 1, 7–10, 12, 19–20, 52,
        56, 75, 77, 87, 97, 106, 109, 113
    data revolution and, 110–111
    decentralizing of, 107
    demographic, 5–6, 16–23, 44, 51–52,
        60–61, 63, 69, 73, 85, 92, 95–96,
        99–101, 104
    further reading on tools for, 115
    future trends and, 112–113
    hidden Markov model (HHM) and, 61,
        97, 118nn6–8
    income brackets and, 20
    latent classes and, 52
    optimization and, 80, 93
    personalization and, 6–7
    politics and, 113–114
    proactive approach and, 112 (see also
        Proactive approach)
    real-time customer information accrual
        and, 95–96
    recommendation systems and, 92, 99,
        105, 108

rewards programs and, 10–11
support systems and, 7–9, 95, 109
transaction data and, 10, 20
Type I errors and, 110
Type II errors and, 110
Interactions, 112
    adaptive marketing decisions and,
        95–103
    basics of customer-centric marketing
        and, 1–2, 5, 7–8, 16–17, 21, 30
    competitive advantage and, 2
    consumer choice and, 41
    continuous learning and, 95–103
    customer lifetime value (CLV) and, 72,
        75
    latent classes and, 52, 54–55, 57, 60

Kamakura, W., 61
Keane, Michael P., 19
Kim, Byong-Do, 115
Kimberly-Clark, 92–93

Latent classes, 21
    AARP and, 63–64
    adaptive marketing decisions and,
        103–104
    advertising and, 64
    binary logit choice model and, 53,
        57
    brands and, 61
    consumer demographic linking and,
        60–61
    consumption and, 51–52, 60–61
    continuous learning and, 58,
        103–104
    customer lifetime value (CLV) and,
        64
    customer loyalty and, 61
    customer preferences and, 59, 61
    decision making and, 61
    email and, 52, 63–64
    information and, 52
    interactions and, 52, 54–55, 57, 60

joint estimation of properties for, 59
logit models and, 53–54, 57, 61
maximum likelihood estimation (MLE) and, 54–57, 62
membership determination and, 58
optimization and, 103–104
panel data and, 54, 56–57, 62
price and, 53, 59–61, 72, 74
proactive approach and, 52
promotions and, 52, 60
segmentation and, 51–64
sensitivities and, 51–64
traditional classification approach and, 52–53
transformation trick for, 57
utility and, 51–53, 59, 62
Lattin, James M., 61
Ledolter, Johannes, 61
Li, Shibo, 61, 97
Liechty, John C., 61
Lilien, Gary L., 115
Little, John, 115
Loblaws, 12–14
Logit models
binary logit choice, 34–36, 40–41, 46, 53, 57
consumer choice and, 33–36, 40–42, 44–47
latent classes and, 53–54, 57, 61
multinomial logit choice (MNL), 33–34, 40–42, 44–47
multiple dependent variables and, 42
multivariate logit choice (MVL), 28, 33–34, 41–42, 44, 46–47
single dependent variables and, 42
Long data, vii, 109–111, 113
Loyalty programs, 43, 107

Mail, 28, 52, 96
Management, vii-viii, 4–5, 8–9, 19, 92, 96–97, 110
Marginal costs, 77, 79, 82–83, 90

Marketing Information Revolution, The (Blattberg, Glazer, and Little), 115
Maximum likelihood estimation (MLE)
consumer choice and, 34, 36, 38, 44–46, 118n5
latent classes and, 54–57, 62
segmentation and, 54–57
sensitivities and, 54–57
Microsoft Dynamics CRM, 9
Mobile apps, 7, 12–13
Montgomery, Alan L., 61, 97
Moon, Sangkil, 61
Multinomial logit choice (MNL) model, 33–34, 40–42, 44–47
Multiple dependent variables, 42
Multivariate logit choice (MVL) model, 28, 33–34, 41–42, 44, 46–47

Neslin, Scott A., 115
Net present value (NPV), 20, 65
Netzer, Oded, 61
Nonprofit associations, 63

Obama, Barack, 113–114
Offshoring, 29–32, 101, 103
On-Demand Customer Relationship Management, 8–9
Open source platforms, 49
Optimization, 4, 21
adaptive learning and, 85, 95–103
advertising and, 93
Amazon and, 92
brands and, 93
bucket pricing and, 23
consumption and, 77–79, 82–91
continuous learning and, 95–103
coupons and, 93
cross-selling and, 27
customer lifetime value (CLV) and, 72, 77–91, 110
customer preferences and, 92
customer response and, 85
decision making and, 7, 77

Optimization (continued)
  dynamic, 4–5, 8–9, 15–18, 21, 23, 26–28,
    30, 32, 72, 83, 85, 89, 95, 97–103, 110,
    118n7
  email and, 92
  forward-looking orientation and, 4–5,
    8–9, 77, 80, 109–111
  Gaussian distribution and, 78
  information and, 80, 93
  Kimberly-Clark and, 92–93
  latent classes and, 103–104
  marginal costs and, 77, 79, 82–83, 90
  OLS analysis and, 78
  price and, 85
  profit and, 78–83, 87–89, 91
  promotions and, 83, 91–93
  regression analysis and, 78
  segmentation and, 77, 85, 91–92
  service call allocation and, 30
  utility and, 77–78, 82–90
  validation and, 87–91
  win-back strategies and, 26
Ordinary least squares (OLS) analysis, 74,
    78

Panel data
  adaptive marketing decisions and, 103
  consumer choice and, 33, 36–38
  continuous learning and, 103
  equal length, 56–57
  latent classes and, 54, 56–57, 62
  segmentation and, 54, 56–57, 62
  time-series, 56
Passive learning, 99–100, 106
PC Plus, 12–14
Phone canvassing, 113
Price
  adaptive marketing decisions and, 96,
    98, 105–106
  basics of customer-centric marketing
    and, 1, 7, 18, 21–24, 25t
  bucket pricing and, 22–24, 25t, 32
  competition and, 112

  consumer choice and, 34, 42–45
  continuous learning and, 96, 98,
    105–106
  discounts and, 34, 43–44, 63, 74–75, 96,
    105
  latent classes and, 53, 59–61, 72, 74
  optimization and, 85
  quality and, 18, 21, 24, 26, 31, 43, 98,
    118
  sensitivities and, 53, 59–61, 72, 74
Principles of Marketing Engineering (Lilien,
    Rangaswamy, and De Gruyn), 115
Proactive approach
  adaptive learning and, 17
  adaptive marketing decisions and, 98,
    106
  continuous learning and, 98, 106
  customer lifetime value (CLV) and, 72,
    75
  decision making and, 1, 4, 6, 9, 15–17,
    20, 22, 26, 29, 31, 52, 72, 75, 98, 106,
    109–110, 112
  latent classes and, 52
  marketing framework for, 15–17, 20, 22,
    26, 29, 31
Profit
  adaptive marketing decisions and, 97–98,
    101, 105
  basics of customer-centric marketing
    and, 1–10, 16, 19–32
  continuous learning and, 97–98, 101, 105
  customer lifetime value (CLV) and,
    66–75, 97–98
  long-term, 1, 5–6, 8, 16, 19–20, 27–30,
    82, 98, 109–111
  optimization and, 78–83, 87–89, 91
  promotions and, 75
  short-term, 5–6, 111–112
Promotions
  adaptive marketing decisions and, 96
  casino industry and, 9–11
  consumer choice and, 41, 49
  continuous learning and, 96

coupons and, 12–14, 20, 44, 73–75, 93,
112
cross-selling and, 6, 22, 26–29, 32, 41,
64, 97, 99
customer lifetime value (CLV) and,
74–75
educating customers and, 6, 28, 61, 97
email and, 3, 6, 28–29, 52, 63–64, 74–75,
92, 96, 113–114
Kimberly-Clark and, 92–93
latent classes and, 52, 60
optimization and, 83, 91–93
personalized, 1
profit and, 75
retention actions and, 13
sensitivities and, 52, 60
supermarkets and, 12–14

Quality
product, 18, 21, 43
service, 24, 26, 31, 98, 118

Rangaswamy, Arvind, 115
RapidMiner, 106
Recommendation systems, 92, 99, 105,
108
Regression analysis
consumer choice and, 33–34, 39, 45–46
customer lifetime value (CLV) and,
72–74
goodness of fit and, 39
optimization and, 78
ordinary least squares (OLS), 74, 78
Relay Foods, 74–75
Returns on investment, 7, 28, 64, 87, 92
Rewards programs, 10–11

Salesforce, 8–9
SAS, 106
Segmentation
AARP and, 63–64
adaptive marketing decisions and, 95,
99–104, 107

basics of customer-centric marketing
and, 2, 5–8, 11–12, 15, 17–22, 27–28,
32
consumer demographic linking and,
60–61
continuous learning and, 40, 49, 95,
99–104, 107
dynamic, 27, 60
email and, 52, 63–64
forward-looking orientation and,
111
hidden Markov model (HHM) and,
118n6
latent classes and, 51–64
maximum likelihood estimation (MLE)
and, 54–57
optimization and, 77, 85, 91–92
panel data and, 54, 56–57, 62
result interpretation and, 59–60
static, 20, 52, 110
traditional classification approach and,
52–53
unobserved, 51
Self-service, 96
Sensitivities
AARP and, 63–64
binary logit choice model and, 53, 57
brands and, 61
consumer demographic linking and,
60–61
customer loyalty and, 61
customer preferences and, 59, 61
decision making and, 61
latent classes and, 51–64
maximum likelihood estimation (MLE)
and, 54–57
panel data and, 54, 56–57, 62
price and, 53, 59–61, 72, 74
promotions and, 52, 60
traditional classification approach and,
52–53
Service calls, 22, 29, 101
Service centers, 31, 101

Service plans, 7, 22–24, 25t
Single dependent variables, 42
Smart phones, 7, 12–14, 22–24, 32, 34, 45, 107
Social media, 6, 49, 74, 96, 114
Solver program, 38–39, 57, 74
Spot offers, 13
Srinivasan, Kannan, 61
Sun, Baohong, 97
Supermarkets, 12–14, 74–75
Support systems, 7–9, 95, 109

Technology
  adaptive marketing decisions and, 96, 105–106
  basics of customer-centric marketing and, 2, 7–11
  consumer choice and, 49
  continuous learning and, 96, 105–106
  customer relationship management (CRM) and, 8–9, 17f, 57, 65, 97–100
  databases and, 8–11, 49, 64, 109, 112–115
  decision making and, 8–9, 113
  digital, 2, 105
  email, 3, 6, 28–29, 52, 63–64, 74–75, 92, 96, 113–114
  investing in, 112
  mobile apps and, 7, 12–13
  open source, 49
  smart phones, 7, 12–14, 22–24, 32, 34, 45, 107
  social media and, 6, 49, 74, 96, 114
  storage, 2
Tepper School of Business, ix
Tesco, 107
Total Rewards program, 10
Transaction data, 10, 20
Triggers, 2, 6, 11, 85, 97

Utility
  adaptive marketing decisions and, 104
  augmenting, 42–44

basics of customer-centric marketing and, 15–16, 21
binary logit choice model and, 53, 57
consumer choice and, 33–35, 39, 41–44, 46–47
continuous learning and, 104
latent classes and, 51–53, 59, 62
linear assumptions and, 35
optimization and, 77–78, 82–90
random, 34–35, 41, 46, 53

Virgin Atlantic, 114

Wachovia, 64
Web analytics (WA), 8
Win-back strategies, 24–26, 32
Wolpin, Kenneth I., 19